Vol. 3

# YES, GOD!

**DEEP LOSS.
GREAT GAIN.**

Vol. 3

# YES, GOD!

MICHELE NOEL-PEAKE

publish your gift

**YES, GOD! VOLUME 3**
Copyright © 2025 Michele Noel-Peake

All rights reserved.

Published by Publish Your Gift®
An imprint of Purposely Created Publishing Group, LLC

No part of this book may be reproduced, distributed or transmitted in any form by any means, graphic, electronic, or mechanical, including photocopy, recording, taping, or by any information storage or retrieval system, without permission in writing from the publisher, except in the case of reprints in the context of reviews, quotes, or references.

Scriptures marked NIV are taken from the New International Version®. Copyright © 1973, 1978, 1984, 2011 by Biblica, Inc.™. All rights reserved.

Scriptures marked NKJV are taken from the New King James Version®. Copyright © 1982 by Thomas Nelson. All rights reserved.

Printed in the United States of America
ISBN (print): 978-1-64484-658-2
ISBN (ebook): 978-1-64484-659-9

---

Special discounts are available on bulk quantity purchases by book clubs, associations and special interest groups. For details email: sales@publishyourgift.com or call (888) 949-6228.
*For information log on to:* www.PublishYourGift.com

# Dedication

This book is dedicated to my Lord and Savior Jesus Christ. It is also dedicated to my mom, Evelyn Noel, and my late husband, Rodney Peake, who are both resting peacefully in our Savior's arms.

I am so glad I said yes to you, Rod, over forty years ago and every time since then until you made your transition to Heaven. Miss you more than words can describe. So grateful God joined us together and blessed us to grow in Him together! Love you always!

Mom, I love and miss you so much and I am so grateful for your example, your love, and your heart that helped to shape me into the Godly woman I am today. Continue to rest well with sweet Jesus.

I also dedicate this book to the best daughters a mom could ever ask for: Zarina and Nia, and my handsome grandson, Zavala! I am super proud of you all and pray God's very best for your futures as your "Yes" to Him continues for a lifetime into eternity.

# Table of Contents

Foreword .................................... ix
Acknowledgements ......................... xiii

Introduction .................................. 1

A Blessing in Disguise
*Catherine Ferrell* ............................ 5

The Sun Will Shine Again
*Ronda Jennings Morrow* ...................... 21

A Minor Setback:
A Lesson in Hope, Strength, and Resilience
*Terri P. Guess* .............................. 35

Finding Love in Unexpected Circumstances
*Porsha S. Harrell* ........................... 51

When the Sun Goes Down
*Imogene Van Buren Burke* .................... 65

It's Still "Yes" in the Deep!
*Michele Noel-Peake* ......................... 79

Conclusion .................................. 95

About the Authors ........................... 97

# Foreword

It is with heartfelt gratitude that my dear sister would think that I am worthy enough to write the foreword for Yes, God! Volume 3. For that reason alone, I am humbled and thankful for this opportunity. Michele Noel-Peake has been and is an integral part of my journey. She is a woman after God's own heart, a prayer champion, my mentor, and my confidant. Michele is a true friend who has always seen the best in me and pushed me to be all that God is calling me to be. Her willingness to be a sounding board with love and support without judgement is a key quality of her relationship with Christ. So, when I was asked to write this foreword, I immediately said "YES" without a second thought.

Michele's walk with Christ exemplifies her love for Him. She has suffered many losses in her lifetime but through it all she remains faithful to her calling. Her strength and tenacity comes from our Heavenly Father. Her ability to push past many obstacles with the help of our Savior has been a beacon of hope for those around her. Even amid the biggest loss of her life, she perseveres with obedience, and for that God will grant her the desires of her heart. Hebrews 11:6 says, "But without faith it is impossible to please Him, for he who comes to God must believe that He is and that He is a rewarder of those that diligently seek Him." There's favor in her "YES" to God!

The stories that you read in this book are evidence that with loss God provides a GAIN. You will see that while enduring loss, these authors may have experienced some form of grief . . . but God! Most often when you think of grief, it's associated with the loss of life; however, there are all sorts of loss that can cause grief. According to Webster's dictionary, grief means "deep and poignant distress caused by or as if by bereavement, a cause of such suffering and trouble, annoyance." I can truly say that I have experienced many causes of grief such as death of a marriage, and loss of loved ones, jobs, friendships, etc. But through every experience, God has been my anchor. Whenever I said "YES" to God, I experienced some type of hardship or loss, but at the same time God would provide me with a great gain.

One of the hardest losses for me was the death of my marriage. Although one may say that's not the same as physical death, I beg to differ. When you make a covenant before God and become one with your husband and a break happens within that covenant, there's a spiritual separation that causes a loss. You are no longer one and a significant part of you dies. This creates some of the same emotions as if there is a physical death. I remember feeling sad, hurt, angry, embarrassed, and ashamed. I felt like a failure. I had so many questions for God like, "Why did this have to happen to me?" and "What did I do to deserve this?"

I recall going to church and rushing out after service because I didn't want anyone to ask questions about the whereabouts of my husband. It took every ounce of strength to get me out of the house for church or any family function that would open me up to questions. Some days all I wanted to do was sleep. I soon realized that I was in a dark pit. My days were up and down like a roller coaster. It became clear to me that I was grieving the death of my marriage.

Although I had no regrets of my decision to leave the marriage, it still did not erase the fact that he had been a part of my life for twenty years. It took much prayer and trusting in God to move forward. The grieving process was not easy, but it was necessary. I pushed through. It was through this loss that I discovered who God was calling me to be. It made me examine myself and address some unresolved issues from my past. I had to heal from past hurts and unanswered questions to move forward.

I grew up not knowing my biological mother and father. It was during this process that I realized that in some ways I had been grieving my entire life, longing for my parents. As a part of my healing, I located my mother and decided to go meet her. Although I had suffered a loss, God gave me my heart's desire—I gained a relationship with my mother.

A few years later, I suffered another loss that changed the trajectory of my future. I lost my job with only a forty-eight hours' notice. This loss was devastating, and it caused me to make a drastic decision. I decided to relocate back home to South Carolina close to family. I had so many mixed emotions and questions once again about how I'd gotten into this predicament. You see, I had been an exemplary employee, but an envious manager decided I was no longer needed. Little did he know that he was setting me up for the biggest comeback. I moved and received an even better job. In addition, I found out who my father was. Although he was deceased, I finally had a name. All the questions I had about my adoption and why my father didn't come for me were answered.

So you see, throughout my life, all the losses I experienced were followed by some great gains that helped shape and mold me into the person God is calling me to be. No matter what happens in life, we are in a win-win situation if we keep our faith in God and trust that He has our best interest in mind. We can rest knowing that His promises are true and He will not withhold any good thing from us.

Sometimes the battle may seem hard, but there's victory on the other side. Keep showing up and doing the work. God will give you double for your trouble. Trusting in the power of God is your SUPERPOWER!

Repeat after me, "God, I trust You." And remember, there's purpose on the other side of the process!

Peace and blessings!

—Tammy L. Woodard

# Acknowledgements

Thank You, Lord, for laying Your life down for us. Thank You, Lord, for never leaving nor forsaking us. Thank You, Lord, for loving us so much that You would die so that we can live life abundantly. What an honor to partner with You in this body of work with the amazing brothers and sisters who have traveled this path of "Yes, God" with me.

Words cannot express my gratitude toward You, Lord, for choosing us to fulfill this divine assignment. I am so grateful to all of the authors between volumes 1 and 3. I pray Your continual favor over all of our lives as we continue on this journey of living lives in pursuit of You, GOD, no matter what may come our way!

I would like to thank every single reader, listener, and supporter who has taken this journey with us. Without you, this would not be possible. Know that you are appreciated and encouraged to continue to press toward the mark God has set for you.

I'm grateful to all of my close brothers and sisters in Christ that helped to hold me up when I needed to be lifted, those who allowed me to pour into them, and vice versa. I value our relationships, and I love that we can laugh and cry together all at the same time. I thank my God for you!

# Introduction

Losing my husband and high school sweetheart after thirty years of marriage and forty years of being together has by far been the single most difficult thing I have gone through in my life. I had been through losses of various kinds before, but there was something so different about this loss that ran so deep for me that I could not put it into words. I simply had this overwhelming thought—how could anyone go through this much pain from a loss and not experience something great from GOD!? Hence, the birth of this book. The third volume of Yes, GOD! Deep Loss. Great Gain.

At first, I thought, *I won't write a chapter because my grief is so new. It's only been a few months.* But I could hear GOD saying, "Go ahead and I will be with you every step of the way. Just trust Me." So this book has been written by faith. Trusting God through the clouds that He has a purpose and a mission for me and the authors of this book and even you, the reader. God has a plan for us all. He tells us in Jeremiah 29:11 that His plans are not to harm us, but to prosper us. And even though it may be hard to see the prosper part sometimes, because of our situation and circumstances, we have to believe Him by faith.

So, the journey began to find others who would have the courage to share their experiences of deep loss and great gain from God. People that at one point in their journey with deep loss felt the same or similar to what I was feeling. People not afraid to say, "I was hurt. I was disappointed. I was devastated. I didn't know at times if I would make it through or not . . . but, God!"

I'm so glad God led me to these powerful and mighty women of GOD who opened up and shared their deep losses in a way that connects us through our human experiences. I am excited for you to read about their unique stories and testimonies of how God literally carried them through deep losses into gains so great only He Himself could provide, heal, and deliver.

Our prayer, collectively and individually, is that you will read each story and find the kind of hope that can only come from the sovereign God of eternity. That no matter where you are in your journey of grief and healing, you will find Him in it.

This book is intended to inspire, encourage, and provide hope to the one on the verge of giving up. The one who is feeling overwhelmed and stricken by grief and depression. We want to say, hold on. Don't give up. With God, you can make it. Life may be different moving forward, but the Master already knew about it, and He has your provisions in the palm of His hands. Psalm 34:18 tells us that God is near to the brokenhearted. It's true. I found out for myself as have the five other writers in this book!

We ask that you please try GOD if you haven't yet. Please don't give up on God when you don't understand what's happening. Please cling to Him even more. No one will ever understand your situation, your pain, your destiny, and your life like the one who created you. God does not want you to go through your loss alone or without Him. He promises to give us beauty for ashes.

—Minister Michele Noel-Peake

# A Blessing in Disguise

*Catherine Ferrell*

*"And we know that in all things God works for the good of those who love Him, who have been called according to His purpose."*—Romans 8:28

## A DIFFERENT KIND OF BATTLE

It felt like the rug had been pulled out from under me. My husband and I sat staring at the screen as we analyzed the lab report and confirmed some of the terminology. I think we both quietly knew, but actually *seeing* the word "cancer" shook me internally like an earthquake. I was numb and in disbelief.

*Me? Cancer?* I thought to myself.

"I don't need to read any more. We'll get the full details from the doctor during the appointment," I said stoically to my husband.

The rest of that night is a blur. I really don't remember much of anything at all.

The time had come. My husband and I sat across the desk from the doctor, maneuvering the chairs in the tight space on our side, to finally discuss this dreaded lab report. When I initially spoke with this doctor, it was the result of a referral stemming from a visit to my primary doctor's office. My nurse practitioner actually generated this referral herself to see this gynecologist. Referrals were normally handled at the front desk when you departed. The nurse also advised me of the lengthy amount of time it may take to get an appointment with this gynecologist—possibly a couple of months or so. She added if that were the case, to let her know and she would perform the examination for me, which really wasn't my preference under the circumstances.

When I returned home, I called the office number provided in the referral, already expecting to receive a long-term appointment date. The young lady answering the phone had great customer service skills. She proceeded to ask me detailed questions about my symptoms and then asked if I could come in. If I recall accurately, it was only about two or three days as opposed to two or three months! After confirming the appointment date, she proceeded to tell me that *she* was the doctor! How about that! This was actually her practice, and it *just so happened* that *she* picked up the phone at the very time I called. She said this wasn't the normal routine, but she just couldn't make patients wait that needed to be seen. That was my initial conversation with this doctor. Little did I know, *God was already showing me favor—first with the nurse and then with the gynecologist.*

Now here we are, sitting across the desk from the gynecologist. Reviewing the medical report at home prior to the appointment helped lessen the sting, as I had time to process the information in my own space. I was now here in her office and intently hanging on to her every word, waiting for the dreaded "C word," but it never came. Someone had to say it, so I did.

"Are you saying cancer?" I asked. (I needed to hear it.)

"Yes," she said, as she nodded.

I have since learned that some doctors prefer not to use the "C word." I imagine it's because the word carries such weight and impact for patients. Perhaps not saying the word helps to diminish some of its perceived power from an emotional perspective. Sometimes I can still barely say it myself, let alone hear it, without having it prick my own emotional scar.

The next steps were set in motion, starting with scheduling a meeting with the recommended gynecologic oncologist. She had already made the call to begin the process, which I appreciated. I've faced challenges before—deadlines, tough negotiations—but this, this was a different kind of battle. It wasn't something I could outthink, outwork, or outbid. This was a mountain that no amount of corporate skill could move.

## MY IDENTITY

I spent most of my adult life in the financial sector, immersed in the corporate world with its perks, pressures, and demands. My career wasn't just a job; it helped shape my identity, values, and goals. I thrived in a dynamic, fast-paced industry—commuting, closing deals, and managing portfolios, all while trying to balance my career and my family. The recognition and sense of being needed was gratifying, and deadlines took precedence. Hard work and achievement were my pride, and I took the trust of my clients and colleagues seriously. I see now that I was building my identity on my expertise, being capable and successful in the world's eyes. God, however, had a greater purpose—one rooted not just in recognition or achievement, but in something deeper and more enduring.

## "WHY ME?"

*Why me?* I thought occasionally. Even my friends and colleagues exclaimed, "Not *you*, Cathy. You eat so healthy!" It's as if they were really saying, "If it can happen to you, then what about the rest of us?"

I do have a healthy respect and deep passion for the incredible benefits of whole foods. Researching, preparing, learning, and sharing knowledge about foods, herbs, spices, and their medicinal properties not only fascinates me, but it awakens something in me. I've even had a taste of foraging along the way—finding edible treasures as close as your own backyard, proving that not all weeds are just weeds (but that's a story for another day). While food isn't the only factor, it's undoubtedly a major factor in fighting disease. Food is medicine—a truth I deeply *feel.* I firmly believe that many of the food-related choices I incorporated throughout the years fortified my body to help endure both the disease and its treatment from a place of greater strength.

Prior to this diagnosis, I was in control of my job, my schedule, my health, and my life plans, or so I thought before being jolted into reality. The harder I tried to hold on, to create some sense of normalcy, the more I succumbed to the fact that I'm not in control. I'm not even in control of my very life. If God, in His infinite wisdom, allowed this disease into my life, surely there was a reason, a purpose. My role was to trust His plan, walk by faith, and follow His lead.

I remember how I felt when I shared the news of the diagnosis with another friend, who commenced to share their news about a relative that didn't make it. I wasn't strong that day, and it was painful as they continued to talk about their loss. Listening to the details was literally tearing me down. Eventually, I excused myself from the conversation.

*In retrospect, I can now see that sharing the unexpected news of my diagnosis triggered their thoughts of loss and pain, which was now exponentially heightening my own.* I learned a valuable lesson that day which prepared me for conversations with others that would surely come.

*Why me?* I thought occasionally. Well, as one friend would poignantly ask, "Why not you?"

## IT JUST SO HAPPENED . . .

In no time at all, God's compassion poured in like a flood, like rushing waters. He surrounded me with a deluge of kind, caring, and knowledgeable people who played pivotal roles in my journey—both before it began and throughout. I had my immediate family, extended family, church family, ministers, and friends from work and my community, along with an incredible team of oncological and medical professionals. Along the way, He placed remarkable people in my path in unusual ways, including an extraordinary nutritionist.

It just so happened that I couldn't reach my regular hairstylist. It just so happened that a backup stylist in another area was available for a last-minute appointment. And it just so happened that this substitute hairstylist was navigating her own potential cancer diagnosis. As we shared our experiences, she mentioned an incredible nutritionist she was working with and proceeded to call her—after hours. It just so happened that the nutritionist was available and spoke with me over the phone for what felt like two hours, free of charge. Her passion ignited mine. She wasn't your typical nutritionist; she said all the right things at the right time, leaving no doubt that I needed her on my team. Her knowledge, experience, and energy were exactly what I needed.

By the way, it just so happens, we still have a relationship today. And to be clear, *none of this "just so hap-*

*pened."* It was all, without a doubt, orchestrated by God, who was working it all out for *my* good.

Individuals from varying fields were placed in my life from childhood and others came along in my adulthood. Some were even in the cancer treatment field. As only God could orchestrate, my daughter's friend was completing his doctorate . . . in cancer research! Coincidence? Not a chance! Accept it or not, it was preordained. This young man even offered to attend my first gynecological oncologist appointment with our family. He, by the way, had his own testimony. He asked insightful, technical questions and patiently translated the complex oncological terminology into layman's terms for me with biological sketches even.

Others in my support system included survivors as well as those who had loved ones with similar journeys. My family's love and their sacrifice were absolutely incredible, whether driving in from out of town with meals in tow, transporting me, sharing medical tips, praying, adding me to their own churches' prayer lists, or just making me laugh when I really didn't want to. God even sent strangers from the most unexpected places, each with the right message at exactly the right time.

Little did I know years before what was ahead for me and how God had already assembled an actual *army* to surround me. For each and every one of them, I am forever grateful.

In addition to spiritual warriors, God provided exceptional medical teams with compassionate staff.

Among them were believers, including one doctor who prayed over me during a critical moment when my treatment schedule was suddenly interrupted for a potentially serious issue. She prayed "God, please let my sister be ok." Prayer warriors lifted me up, both domestically and across the globe, many of whom I may never meet. Closer to home, people shared their testimonies, experiences, and insights, pouring into me in ways that strengthened me physically, emotionally, and most importantly, spiritually. As I prepared for chemotherapy, I leaned on their wisdom—listening, reading, researching, and consulting with doctors and acquaintances. Every piece of advice, no matter how small, was invaluable in helping me navigate this journey. Most of all, I learned the importance of surrounding myself with positive, encouraging people, many of whom prayed with me and for me.

## CHEMO DOESN'T DISCRIMINATE

It was not a good day. I was lying on the living room floor in front of the piano, curled into a fetal position. "Don't touch me," I said. "Just leave me here." My legs were in excruciating pain. Sometimes, the treatment felt worse than the diagnosis itself. Even now, at times it's hard to write, hear, or say the word out loud—I often just call it "the diagnosis." Surgeries were behind me, and I was now in the chemotherapy phase. Each cycle of infusions brought its share of ups and downs. But when the bad days hit, they came with a vengeance. *Chemo, after all, doesn't discriminate; it targets both the bad and the good cells.*

Interestingly enough, it generally wasn't the chemo itself, but the pre- and post-treatment medications meant to manage side effects that hit the hardest. The pain in my legs, the overwhelming exhaustion, and the absence of the God-given *joy of taste* are memories that linger. One of my warriors had warned me this could happen. My body felt like it had betrayed me—my taste buds yielding only metallic bitterness or no taste at all. Even my sense of smell turned against me.

## THINK ABOUT WHAT YOU'RE THINKING ABOUT

During the very early stages of this diagnosis, I recall a few times where I would briefly consider those "what if" thoughts. I thought I was being logical and considering potential outcomes. However, these thoughts would go straight down the rabbit hole—even to the point of picturing a body in a casket at a funeral. I recall years ago one of my daughters saying "what if" statements are generally thoughts that end with negative results. Even though I wasn't seeing it this way at the moment, they really are an expression of fear and anxiety. It's important to be aware of our thought lives so that they don't take on lives of their own. Negative thoughts are counterproductive on many levels. Once aware, I examine them for any merit and replace them with positive thoughts or Scriptures—the living, breathing, cutting and healing Word of God.

There are some cognitive studies that suggest *people can have anywhere from 6,000 to 80,000 thoughts per day, with 70-80 percent of those thoughts tending to be negative or self-critical. I've seen similar statistics over the years, and all are astounding.* Now, that's food for thought!

Around this time, still in the very early stages of the diagnosis, I had a very interesting conversation with a relative and minister, whom my sister asked to contact me. She not only talked with me, but she also prayed for me and suggested I create a list of affirmations. That was already on my mind, so she was really confirming that I had to move forward now. She reminded me that I had to *see* myself as healed, imagine my very *cells* as healthy, *and see myself the way God designed me.* This process was the exact opposite of those "what if" thoughts.

I prepared a list of scriptural affirmations, posting it on my wall where I saw and read it daily as I arose each morning. I even included pictures of joyful family occasions and a future trip to Egypt. Those affirmations and pictures are still on my wall today. I cannot begin to explain the significance those affirmations played in my thought life and in my healing. Another minister and sister encouraged me to read these affirmations aloud during a group prayer meeting to help those in the group with their own health challenges. It was well received. It was powerful. God would bring people into my path for me to help pour into them the same way I was being poured into! I am grateful I was encouraged to start sharing my affirmations.

It was one of many powerful experiences that occurred within the *army God had already lined up to help build and keep me up.*

## WHAT ARE YOU GOING TO DO DIFFERENTLY?

Time and treatments were moving forward. One day my daughter asked me a simple, yet thought provoking question: "What are you going to do differently when you return to work?" I couldn't answer because I had no idea what I would do differently. Would I just dive back into my previous habits? Probably so. I know what needs to be done at work, so I go into autopilot mode, and I get the job done whether it's demands from the deal at hand or demands from myself. It's part of my makeup.

Gradually, I was starting to realize that my rush to close deals, the pressure to meet deadlines, and the constant need to prove myself were also distractions. My relationship with God, with family, and even with myself had taken a backseat to my career on more than one occasion.

Would I change? If so, what would I change? How would I change? I couldn't answer. I didn't answer, though the question would replay like a song that continues to worm its way in and out of your mind, *"What are you going to do differently?"*

Day after day, I endured the effects of the cumulative radiation treatment penetrating a body already stripped of hair from chemotherapy. My skin was now so severely darkened from my waist to my thighs, I just hoped and prayed that it would hold up and not crack nor become infected with each passing treatment. My husband took great care of me, as much as humanly possible, every step of the way. He ensured I had my medicine and food—whenever I could eat—not to mention making early-morning commutes, thirty miles away, for my all-day chemotherapy infusions. He would then go to work and return during evening rush hour traffic to pick me up. He is definitely a soldier and a blessing. But the real blessing is that I have a husband who prays for me.

Sometimes, life *throws mammoth challenges* our way, leaving us standing without a foundation, walking without a clear path. Yet, it is precisely in those moments that *mammoth faith flows in*, bridging the gap between our shortcomings and His boundless grace. The question still echoed in my heart: *"What are you going to do differently?"*

If you had asked me before this diagnosis what my greatest fear was, I would have said losing control—over my career, my future, my health, my independence, and my life choices. But what I once saw as the end of my career and the way of life I had always known turned out to be the beginning of something far more profound. Through this journey, I've come to understand that losing control, control that we really never had, isn't the worst thing that can happen. In fact, it may be the best thing that can happen when Jesus Christ, the Good Shepherd, is the one guiding our steps.

## YEA, THOUGH I WALK THROUGH THE VALLEY OF THE SHADOW OF DEATH, I WILL FEAR NO EVIL FOR YOU ARE WITH ME . . .

Throughout this journey, I found myself deeply connected with Psalm 23. Verse four of this Psalm has a story of its own: While lying on the flat radiation table each day, I would close my eyes and silently recite each verse, one after another. I would reflect on each verse, interpreting its meaning as I went along. At times, my thoughts would drift—wondering if I missed or repeated a verse—or I would pause to just reflect on the meaning of a particular verse. This daily routine became a way for me to escape the harsh reality of the radiation beams targeting my body. By the time I reached the final verse, the treatment was usually done. If not, I would simply start over.

I remember waking up at home one sunny Saturday morning and *verse four* just took on a life of its own. I sat on the edge of the bed looking at the beauty of the trees in the backyard through my bedroom window. The blue sky and the green grass created a natural backdrop for a perfect picture. As I looked, I noticed the daily morning shadow cast by our rooftop over an area of the yard. I stared at the shadow as it was slowly shrinking, and the light began shining brighter. The shadow instantly reminded me of the powerful words in Psalm 23:4: *Yea, though I walk through the valley of the shadow of death, I will fear no evil for you are with me . . .*

Yea, though I *walk . . .*

The Word says, "I w*alk."* It does not say I'm stuck or that I'm stagnant in my circumstances. It says, "I *walk."* I'm physically *moving* through this journey.

What's more is that it does not just say that I walk—it says, "I walk *through."* The word *through* is important here because it shows movement—passing from one side to another. It's a process, a transition. "*Through*" also indicates that this journey is continuing, progressing toward completion. When I am "*walking through,"* I am trusting and believing that when I reach the other side, when I complete this journey, the Good Shepherd will have already worked things out for my good.

"*The valley*" reminds me of my visit to the Dead Sea in the Jordan Rift Valley years ago. It's literally the lowest point on the surface of the earth where no aquatic life survives *today*, yet the Word prophesies that one day the salty waters will become fresh and overflowing with life. Despite the joys and challenges, He's on the mountain and He's in the valley. He's restoring me, protecting me, and guiding me. I'm blessed to walk through the valley because He's permitted it.

"*The shadow of death*" is not death itself but merely its shadow. Shadows require three items: light, an object on which the light shines, and a surface to catch the shadow. A shadow, in and of itself, has no power. It's simply the result of the interaction between the light and an object. The shadow cannot exist without light, nor can it have any true power over us. In the same way, God's presence transforms the darkness into light. His light removes fear and confusion, and it brings clarity, understanding, and hope. John 1:5 says, "The light shines in the darkness, and the darkness has not overcome it." The shadow only exists because of the light, and it has no power to control us when the light of God is with us and within us. *Darkness flees.*

The verse continues, "*I will fear no evil.*" Why? Because You, Lord, are with me. I will not fear the depth of the valley, the powerlessness of the shadow, or even death itself because You are with me. Wherever I go, You are there, and You promised You would never leave me nor forsake me. I feel Your presence. You are with me, and *in You*, I place my trust.

## A BLESSING IN DISGUISE

I began to see that my life was already shifting. My health moved to the forefront, while my career began to take a step back. God spoke to me in ways I had never experienced before. There's a saying: "Sometimes when God wants your attention, He'll whisper—but if you don't listen, He'll shout." I don't believe He was shouting, but I do know He was serious. I believe now that He allowed this trial to reshape me, to rewire my perspective, and to draw me into a deeper, richer relationship with Him. Through it all, I've gained far greater than I ever would have imagined.

This journey has also reignited my passion regarding the intricacies of nutrition and its amazing capabilities, a gift I continue to explore with gratitude. Though treatments have depleted some of my body's resources, I am joyfully focusing on replenishing and rebuilding. Challenges remain, but I live with peace, joy, and a renewed sense of purpose.

Through surrender and trust, I've come to understand that for everything I lack, God has it all. Walking through my valley by faith and not by sight has brought clarity, strength, and new opportunities, including this book. This has truly been a blessing in disguise.

# The Sun Will Shine Again

*Ronda Jennings Morrow*

It was nearly ten years ago that I was kneeling on the sofa in the hospital room with my son, Jay, next to me as we watched the cars zoom by below on Michigan Avenue in Washington, D.C. We were making small talk about events that had no relevance to the reason we were there in the first place. Neither one of us wanted to talk about what it meant for us to be in that room.

I had spoken to Jay first thing that morning and he told me that Jayde, his twenty-one-month-old daughter and my granddaughter, still was not feeling well after two weeks of going back and forth to the doctor. She had been having nose bleeds and was lethargic, so the first thought was that she was allergic to pollen because after all it was allergy season. But that last doctor's visit revealed something much more sinister was going on. That early morning call would not only change the course of our day but our lives forever. Acute megakaryoblastic leukemia or its street name, AML-M7.

On the morning of May 20, 2014, Jayde had been taken from her doctor's office by ambulance straight to the hospital where my son and I waited for her arrival. We knew something was not right when we arrived in the emergency room and they said she already had a room.

## Yes, God!

We looked at one another confused. We were just told she was being sent to the hospital. Why would she already have a room?

While sitting in the room with our family as we looked across at the hospital doctors, it became clear why Jayde had a room upon arrival. The fear of her personal doctor was being confirmed. Jayde had leukemia. I remember thinking, *What kind of foolishness are these people talking about*? "These people" meaning the doctors. Not only did she have leukemia, but she had a rare form of leukemia that, at the time, only gave her about a 20 percent chance of survival. Lord! How did we get here?!

I am a solution-oriented person and very Type A, so one of my first statements after feeling like I had just gotten hit in the chest by a ton of bricks was to ask how we can fix it. Please take note of all the personal pronouns I use throughout my narrative. You will see that I was ready to take charge and put the world back on its axis. It was obvious to me that the moon and sun were not in alignment with Pluto or some other planet because I felt my world crashing down around me. I heard "Blah, blah, blah, blah, blah." My only thoughts were: *How do we make this all better? This is my granddaughter. This is my first and only grandchild. I need this to be resolved. Now. Stat.*

The family was given a treatment plan for Jayde which required her to spend most of her time in the hospital. We were also told we could bring things from home and decorate her room. Of course, me being Mimi (which is what she called me), I left the hospital and went straight to Walmart. I knew she loved Minnie Mouse and Doc McStuffins, so I went into the store to buy every toy I thought would bring a smile to her face because she did not feel well, and she was not happy to be in the hospital.

Jayde was very selective about who she liked to have in her presence, and she found herself in a strange place with people that wanted to touch her and stick her with things that caused her discomfort and pain. As her Mimi, it was unbearable to see her upset. I felt incredibly helpless since I could not make things better for her. There were times I had to leave the room and go as far away as I could so that I could not hear her cry. My heart would break into tiny pieces when I heard her scream. I felt like I was letting her down because I could not make the pain stop and those little eyes were saying "help me." What use was I? Why could I not fix this?

For nearly eight months, Jayde fought leukemia as best she could. But on January 12, 2015, at two years old, she said goodbye to this world forever. I had felt in my spirit for a couple of weeks before her passing that she would not win her battle on this side of Heaven, but my heart was in denial.

I say that because my husband and I had gone to see her on a Saturday two weeks prior. The room was filled with visitors that day. I cannot remember who else was there besides her parents and my husband and I, but there were others. I do remember that Jayde was in a mostly good mood, eating popsicles, and holding court. Did I mention that we called her Lady Jayde because of her sassy and entitled demeanor from the moment she was born?

Well anyway, that day she was holding court while her faithful servants were in a semi-circle around her as she ate her popsicles. She suddenly began calling out the names of those who were in the room. As she called each person's name, she waited until they acknowledged her. Then, she said, "I love you," and moved on to the next person. At that moment, I felt in my spirit that was her way of telling us goodbye.

That moment reminded me so much of the Saturday before my mom had passed. It was a good visit with my mom and the room was full of visitors. We laughed and joked that day, and on the following Monday morning, I received a phone call saying she was gone. When Jayde went around that room and shared her love with everyone, that memory came flooding back. I wanted to smile and cry at the same time. I dared not speak the words that I was feeling into the universe because to me that would mean they would come true.

On the ride home, I sat in the passenger seat silently looking out the window as though I was in a trance. Suddenly my husband broke the silence. He said, "She was telling us goodbye, wasn't she?" My only response was, "Yes," as I felt my chest grow heavy with unshed tears. I finally began to accept that she might not be with us long.

There was a mix of emotions immediately after Jayde's passing. On the one hand, I was relieved that she was no longer in pain when even a simple kiss on the forehead had caused her to cry out in pain. My prayers had turned from, "Lord, please save her" to "Lord, may Your holy will be done" because I did not want her to suffer any longer. On the other hand, that was when the clouds began to descend around me. I did not realize how much I had been trying to keep it together for Jayde's sake, her parents' sake, and for the sake of our family.

I was a church attending believer and we cannot walk around as those without hope. Right? I had been walking around holding on to that faith the size of a mustard seed for dear life and now the thing I feared most had happened. Jayde's life here on Earth was over, and the fight left my body.

I remember lying in bed feeling as though I didn't have enough strength to inhale and exhale. But I knew I could not give in to those feelings because we still had to officially say goodbye to our princess. I still had to make it through the longest day of my life, the day of the funeral. So, I depended on God to give me my breaths.

The morning of the funeral, I woke up feeling the full weight of the dread of the day. I stood in the shower screaming in my head: *Why my granddaughter?! Why my Jayde?! There were so many things that I had planned for us. She was just two years old. We did not get a chance to have our girls' day out, lunch dates, or playtime at the park*. All the plans I had for her would never come to fruition. I was devastated! Do you recall that I previously said to pay attention to all the personal pronouns I was using? Add these to the list.

Although I felt like I was having an out-of-body experience, I was blessed to be surrounded by incredible people—family, friends, church family, co-workers, hospital workers, strangers, etc.—who were truly uplifting and helped give me strength to make it through that day. The capacity of humanity, when we forget our differences and remember that we are a community, is awe inspiring. The hugs, love, and kindness lifted those clouds intermittently on that day as we celebrated Jayde's limited time in our lives. We shared a meal and stories and laughed and cried. But as the day continued, I began to lose steam. I only wanted to get to my room where I could close the door and lock out the rest of the world. I wanted to just lie down in all my emotions. Lay in all the hurt, pain, and extreme sadness.

I had experienced grief from the loss of my mother, but I had never felt this heaviness before—I did not feel like I could breathe. I do not have the words for that feeling or a description. I am not sure one even exists. The closest I can come is that the color had been removed from my life, and I was now seeing everything in black and white. The vibrant colors like red, orange, and yellow were now gone. The sky was still blue. The birds still sang, but I could no longer see their beauty or hear their songs. Grief had robbed me of my senses.

As I moved through my days, I knew that others could see the colors because I could see the smiles on their faces. But, for the life of me, I could not understand their happiness. Did they not get the memo that Jayde was no longer here? How could they be laughing and exercising and seemingly moving as if they did not have a care in the world when the world was missing a beautiful and sassy two-year-old affectionately called Lady Jayde. I just could not wrap my grief-stricken mind around it.

On a cold morning not long after Jayde passed, I was walking across the U.S. Capitol on my way to work. It had become the norm for me to move through my day like I was on cruise control. I knew the routine by heart and no thought was required. Get up, shower, catch the bus, walk across the Capitol, work a full day, catch the bus home, distract myself with television, then it was bedtime. Wash, rinse, and repeat. Just a bunch of mindless movements. Until that cold morning when the cloud cover that had descended upon me and was now the reason I saw everything in black and white instead of color became too heavy.

I had been watching the people jogging around the Capitol and they seemed happy. I remembered that feeling of happiness, but I could not figure out how to feel it and get it back in my life. I was just sad inside. I continued on my way, putting one foot in front of the other on my memorized path to work that required no thought and no feeling.

Then, I said, "God I need help. I don't want to feel like this anymore." I was numb and wanted to feel like I was still a part of the world. I honestly do not remember whether I felt a change that day or not, but I do know that something inside of me began to move.

It seems that the morning gives me clarity of thought. It is my favorite time of day to talk to God about what is on my mind and in my heart. It was on another early morning walk to work that I heard in my spirit that we should start an organization in Jayde's name. As quickly as the thought appeared, I pushed it out of my mind.

*What do you know about starting an organization? You must have lost your mind.*

I shared my thoughts with my husband and son and was thoroughly disappointed by their responses. They both said it was a good idea. You may wonder why I was disappointed by their affirmative responses, but it was because I was waiting for someone to talk me out of my idea. I was not a medical professional or an expert on pediatric cancer. *I cannot give anyone advice. Who do I think I am?* And just like that, the question was answered. In my mind I heard, "You may not be a medical expert, but you are an expert on being Jayde's grandmother."

Wow, there it was. My last line of defense shattered. I was Jayde's Mimi and I had been in the room. I saw firsthand the hell that many families go through when a child is diagnosed with a life-threatening disease. I witnessed how cancer stole her childish laughter that used to bring so much joy to our ears and replaced it with stoic silence. Many times, her only emotions were those of pain that could come even by a gentle kiss on the forehead. Yeah, I knew what that was like as a grandmother. How I wished I could make it all better for her and her parents while drowning in my own pain and helplessness.

I was indeed an expert at being Jayde's grandmother and I was going to start doing just that again. Although Jayde was no longer physically with me, I was still her grandmother and together we were going to make sure her short two years here on Earth were impactful.

I immediately began to research the type of organization I wanted to have and decided on a 501(c)3 nonprofit. My laptop became my constant companion. If I'm honest, the laptop belonged to my husband, and he had just purchased it for himself around the Christmas holiday. I soon took possession of it, and he did not have the heart to reclaim it for himself. That is something we still laugh about today. Even if we were watching television, I was on that laptop plugging away. I was researching the steps to creating a nonprofit—how do I trademark it? What will be our mission? Etc. I became a woman possessed.

And then, I noticed that something strange had happened in the midst of my focus and mission. I had begun seeing things around me in color again. The heavy gray mist that seemed to envelop me was beginning to lift. My days did not seem so mechanical anymore. I was waking up every day with purpose—ensuring that Jayde's name lived on long after I was gone. I believed wholeheartedly that her purpose among us was greater than just being a daughter, a sister, or a granddaughter. Her short life was not in vain. I believed we were supposed to learn something from this life-altering experience and then we were supposed to do something!

I did not understand at that time that I was working out my grief and that starting an organization to honor Jayde was my grief counseling. All I knew was that I was no longer feeling the hopelessness and helplessness I previously felt. I no longer wanted to be a victim of cancer but a participant in the fight against cancer. I just had to determine what role I wanted to play. Jayde was a warrior, and I too wanted to be a warrior.

Jayde passed on January 12, 2015, and the nonprofit that holds her name and likeness was incorporated on June 1, 2015. We immediately started fundraising. Jayde M. Schools Incorporated's mission is to assist families, in our local community, who are experiencing a pediatric cancer diagnosis with incidentals such as transportation, hospital parking, food, groceries, and other items to help them get through the day. The organization has also assisted families who have lost their child to pediatric cancer with burial assistance. It is understandable that a family that is focusing on hope is not preparing for death.

It is surreal that we are now approaching the tenth anniversary of when Jayde became an angel at just two years old. I do not feel as if that much time has passed. As an individual, and collectively as an extended family, we are still honoring Jayde's legacy by bringing awareness to pediatric cancer and helping others. This is now my life, and I have learned amazing things about myself and my capabilities. I am the person who actively dodged public speaking in high school and college because of the paralysis of fear.

Before Jayde, I proudly professed to be a worker bee— always happy to assist but not a person to take the leading role. My love for Jayde put me front and center, and in the interim, I found my passion. I would never have placed such a bet that I would find my passion standing in front of people speaking. It was once a totally insane thought, but here I am. I still experience anxiety, but the opportunity to share Jayde's story while helping others gives me a supernatural boldness that I did not know I possessed.

Remember how I previously said to pay attention to the personal pronouns I was using— such as: "Why *my* granddaughter?! Why *my* Jayde?"—and all the plans I had made for her? In the middle of my rant, I came to the realization that I had made Jayde's passing all about what had happened to me and how unfair it was to me, as if her purpose on this earth had been solely about being here for me. I kept replaying my life, trying to determine which action or event had sealed her fate. What sin did I commit that caused her to carry such a heavy cross? And then I heard a small voice in my spirit say, "Get over yourself. Chile, you done made this about you."

In my grief and arrogance, I had made it all about me. It had been my conclusion that a child as young as Jayde did not have a purpose separate from the purpose of the adults around them. Wow! Jayde passed through this world and our lives with her own individually assigned purpose. Was it to motivate me, her parents, or her family members? I do not know and can only speculate. What I do believe is that she was an influencer in the lives of those who knew her and those who met her through the recounting of her life.

I also believe that grief can arrest one's passion and purpose if not addressed. I use the word arrest because the definition can mean to stop or check (progress or a process). It is my belief that Jayde's destiny was tied to mine and mine to hers. For me to fulfill my purpose, I had to experience all that was Jayde, which included all the love and all the pain. If I had any foresight into the path that would eventually lead me to my passion, I would have stopped in my tracks and refused to move forward in my life.

Just as Jonah in the Bible had initially declined his assignment to take a message to the people of Nineveh, I too would have refused my assignment if I had known my path would lead to me experiencing the loss of Jayde. I jokingly say that the whale would have had two occupants, me and Jonah. But truthfully, I believe that in God's wisdom and mercy, it is revealed to us only that which we can handle at any given moment.

If Jayde had passed away at any other time in my life, I may not have answered the call to step up and be the person I am today. She was the light that led me to the purpose and passion that resides within me.

There are no words to describe the suffocating stronghold that grief can place on your life. The feelings of hopelessness and despair that leave you searching for the meaning of life and questioning your very existence. Grief leaves you feeling like you are a spectator in your own life, watching yourself from the other side of a mirror. But God! I am thankful every day that I have a relationship with God. Without my faith, I would drown in my emotions for grief has no expiration date and at times shows up in my day unexpectedly. But through my faith, I am constantly reminded that I am not without hope and that one day I will see Jayde again as written in 1 Thessalonians 4:13-18.

I have learned that I am stronger than I could ever have imagined and every day that I open my eyes I have purpose. Part of my purpose is to support families fighting pediatric cancer through our nonprofit. As I like to say when speaking at charity fairs, Jayde left me an assignment. I am now Mimi on a mission, and I take my mission seriously.

# A Minor Setback: A Lesson in Hope, Strength, and Resilience

*Terri P. Guess*

Attentively sitting in church as a child, I distinctly remember the pastor instructing the congregation to not only thank God for waking them up that morning but to thank Him for awaking them with the use of their limbs. I naively thought, *How could someone wake up without the use of their limbs, especially if they were working the night before?* Regardless, I did as I was told.

In 2003, I had an experience likened to the pastor's plea. I awakened not without the use of my limbs but without my full eyesight. Unbeknownst to me this was the beginning of a journey that would test my faith, my physical strength, and my endurance.

At the time, I was well beyond my twenties, beyond the age of thinking I was invincible. I was healthy, but not without the usual health challenges we all face from time to time. My parents were aging. I was progressing in my career. I had a home of my own, a reasonably stable relationship, and friendships to cherish. Overall, life was good.

I simply thought I was suffering from a case of dust, lint, dirt, or hair in my eye. I experienced some pain in movement, but it was minimal. Over the weekend, I rubbed my eye profusely, flushed it, washed it with eye drops, and had my mom blow in it. Nothing helped. Defeated but not hopeless, I continued with my regular routine—going to bed at 12:30 or 1 a.m., up at 6 a.m., driving forty minutes on the parkway to catch the train for a forty-five minute ride to Trenton, then a fifteen minute walk to the office, unless the bus was waiting outside the station.

I continued with this grueling task as my eyesight worsened. Realizing the need to see an ophthalmologist, I was first misdiagnosed with macular degeneration. If that wasn't bad enough, a follow-up phone call determined I had a case of optic neuritis instead and that I should see a neuro-ophthalmologist. Worry began to set in. The term neuro made me nervous, as I recognized its association with the nerves. I immediately got busy on the internet and quickly found that optic neuritis is firmly associated with multiple sclerosis for which there is no cure.

***Optic neuritis is swelling of the eye's optic nerve. The optic nerve carries light signals from the back of your eye to your brain so you can see. If the optic nerve is swollen, damaged, or infected, you cannot see clearly.***

Locating a neuro-ophthalmologist became upsettingly frustrating as they are highly specialized. Navigating the bureaucracy of the healthcare industry coupled with the limitations of an HMO made my head spin. I prayed for an answer to the all-too-familiar questions: What is going on with me? Why is this happening? Will I ever see again? Will I find or get help? My prayers were answered with my introduction to the kindest doctor whose staff was sympathetic to my needs. Upon hearing the desperation in my voice, the nurse gave me an appointment immediately.

The doctor performed a series of tests. I had no idea how well I performed as they were all new to me. After what I perceived to be hours, the doctor entered the room gingerly and cautiously informed me of my biggest fear: I was at risk of having multiple sclerosis. He kindly suggested I see a neurologist for confirmation before following up with him and that in the meantime I go home and rest.

I took some time alone to shed a tear, but I had no time to agonize over the possibility of having multiple sclerosis. I needed confirmation. My priority was to schedule an MRI for a proper diagnosis. While many talked of their claustrophobic experience in the machine, I decided to focus on the importance of getting it done. Fortunately, my first experience in the intimidating machine was fine, as routine visits for an MRI would eventually become common practice.

"How did I do?" I asked the technician. I received a generic yet kind response—"You will have to follow up with your doctor," he said sweetly. So, the waiting game began.

The wait wasn't as long as I expected. The chosen doctor, who lacked decorum, was quite blunt in his delivery. "Your MRI shows that you have MS." Without hesitation, he gave me a prescription for a steroid for what was deemed inflammation in my eye. I took it, hurried home, and said to myself, *Hold up! Wait a minute! Is this my only choice for action?* I took time to gather my thoughts and rationalize between tears and hugging my Biskit, all eighty pounds of a gentle, yellow Labrador.

Up to this point it was just he and I, aside from brief talks with my sorority sister—complaining of my reduced sight—and updating my parents on my perceived limited misfortune.

What the ophthalmologist described as a blind spot became increasingly worse. It was an area in my eye where I could not see clearly. Within a matter of weeks, I lost my peripheral vision. I learned that my optic nerve was damaged and had become inflamed, which is medically described as optic neuritis. Common symptoms of optic neuritis, described by the Mayo Clinic, are pain with eye movement and temporary vision loss.

*Multiple sclerosis can cause numbness, weakness, trouble walking, vision changes and other symptoms. It's also known as MS. In MS, the immune system attacks the protective sheath that covers nerve fibers, known as myelin. This interrupts communication between the brain and the rest of the body.* —Mayo Clinic

Meanwhile, I continued to work, moving back home to get rides to and from the train station from my father and brother, who tried to offer comfort and understanding. But it was my mother I needed—her nurturing touch, the softness of her voice, the sympathy and compassion in her eyes. She was at a church conference at the time. I tried to stay strong, but upon hearing her voice while explaining my ordeal, I simply broke down.

When she returned, she sprang into action, calling people I had not thought to reach out to for further direction. Mom called her brother, the uncle I adore, for his intellect and rationale. He sternly directed me to seek a specialist. "Get a second opinion. Don't take what you first encountered as gospel," he demanded.

I complied without hesitation but not before seeing about my eyes. I had business with the neuro-ophthalmologist. With trepidation, I entered his office with Mom by my side. Before he could ask, I blurted out, "I have MS and the doctor wants to give me a steroid for my eyes!" He took a deep breath and confidently said, "Studies have shown that those with optic neuritis regain their sight just as quickly without a steroid as those who take a steroid."

My eyes surely widened upon hearing the news. He left the decision to take the steroid up to me. I didn't. Instead, I slowed down and changed my lifestyle. I had no other choice. Aside from the toxic work environment I found myself in, I simply came and went, resting more and contemplating.

***Matthew 11:28-30: "Come to me, all you who are weary and burdened, and I will give you rest. Take my yoke upon you and learn from me, for I am gentle and humble in heart, and you will find rest for your souls. For my yoke is easy and my burden is light."***

Rest is exactly what I did. The comfort I received from my Biskit helped; the simple act of stroking his fur was calming. Then, miraculously, one night while lying in bed, a picture that turned gray when I began losing my sight started to brighten. Each day it improved!

As my eyesight improved, I mustered the energy to visit the MS specialist. The office was ominous. There were people there on canes, in wheelchairs, and some walking imbalanced. I was overwhelmed and could have walked out (as my eyesight had improved), but since optic neuritis is associated with MS, I decided to follow through.

I was blessed with another doctor who was kind, gentle, and forthright. After more testing, talking, and listening, I was given the choice to do nothing and wait for the possibility of a second symptom that would definitely confirm a diagnosis or begin a medication to possibly avoid a relapse. It would not be an easy choice. I was also approached by a nurse who exclaimed, "You would be perfect for a study!" where I would be given a placebo. I had a major decision to make. I didn't ponder long and chose medication. The optic neuritis was scary. I didn't want to risk the chance of it happening again.

*Psalm 56:3-4: When I am afraid, I put my trust in you. In God, whose word I praise—in God I trust and am not afraid. What can mere mortals do to me?*

My life was changing, but I was determined to fight. I would not allow the diagnosis or the possibility of becoming disabled to hinder me. Administering the medication required training as I would be giving myself a subcutaneous needle weekly. After practicing by plunging a needle deeply into an orange, I thought I was ready. The feat was easy on a large piece of fruit, my thighs were extremely different. My first attempts were disastrous. The recommended glass of wine did not calm my frayed nerves. I found myself playing with the needle before insertion, thereby infecting it unintentionally. After gaining the nerve to plunge the needle into my skin, I drew quite a bit of blood.

After cleaning up my mess, I jumped into bed, covering myself with a ton of blankets and an extra sheet for Biskit. The side effects were horribly painful: flu-like symptoms coupled with the chills. I did not like the thought of having a dog on my bed, but I needed warmth as I would often awaken shivering and with a headache.

After cleaning many blood-stained floors, I enlisted the help of Mom, who after proper training would make a weekly visit to administer the needle, alternating arms.

I remained on this medication regimen for ten years, until I became immune to the medicine. "What next?"

I asked. The doctor I admired and respected had unexpectedly left the practice. I was given another doctor who was highly respected but advanced in age. He was not impressed with alternative medicine, something I considered exploring. He prescribed another Disease Modifying Therapy (DMT). The recommended drug was an infusion. I had to go to an infusion center and sit for two hours, including a half hour for observation.

***Disease Modifying Therapies (DMTs) can help manage* MS *by reducing relapses and slowing its progression.***

While I am grateful for the DMTs, I was partly dismayed. On the one hand, I was optimistic about the prospect of having access to medication that had the potential to help me. When I was first diagnosed, a nurse offered hope, telling me of a time when there weren't many options for those suffering from MS.

However, I was later informed that DMTs merely slow the progression of the disease. The doctors, nurses, and literature clearly emphasized this information, leaving me less than hopeful. This feeling intensified after I experienced relapses, notably when I lost sight in my other eye, though I recovered more quickly this time.

A most devastating relapse was losing the use of my dominant hand. It became so weak that I could no longer write unless I used a modified pen. To my dismay, I would drop things—a fork, cup, or dish. My cooking became limited and my penmanship, which I took pride in, was slowly getting worse. A steroid was prescribed to help me regain use of my dominant hand quicker. I instead found better healing through regimented occupational therapy. Nevertheless, I remained committed to taking the medication in an effort to prevent becoming disabled.

## Respect the Journey

*A chronic disease can steal away your life.*
*That certainly gives you a reason to gripe.*

*It is devastating to you, your family, and any friend.*
*But that doesn't mean that it has to be the end.*

*Respect the journey, weather the storm.*
*Faith and perseverance won't leave you torn.*

*God is preparing you for the next chapter.*
*Something bigger, something better in the thereafter.*

*So don't worry, don't fret, be happy in the now.*

*Once you complete the task, you will understand and praise. Oh wow! —TPG*

I tried one DMT after another. The slow drip of the two infusions, my next prescribed medication, left me fearful. I became immune to them both. *What am I really putting into my body*, I would ask myself. *Is it really working?* The doctors reassured me it was, stating that my MRIs showed no new lesions.

***An MS lesion (sometimes also called a plaque or scar) is an area in the central nervous system that has been damaged by the immune system's attack. MS lesions are thought to occur upon a backdrop of inflammation.***

In the meantime, I changed doctors. Not only was I dissatisfied with my current doctor but also where he was located. It was recommended that I try a female doctor instead. I was getting along well with her. Unfortunately, in less than a year, she announced that she was leaving the practice. I decided to stay the course with the new doctor who came highly respected.

It was during this time that I began showing visible signs of MS. I became dependent on a cane, but I kept it fashionable—bright purple and red—in an effort to maintain my dignity. I proudly hobbled along hoping my MS would not get any worse.

A rollator was then added to my arsenal as my balance was off. Still fashion conscious, I opted for a faux Burberry that held all my essentials. It was also during this time that I began taking oral medication. With the first oral medication, I had to titrate the doses. After a mix-up in communication and having to restart the titration, I decided against its use.

My last medicinal option left me with a mixed bag of emotions. The amount of testing was intense. My questions went unanswered, or I was given answers that were unsatisfactory. After a year, it also began to lose its effectiveness as I found it difficult to stand and lift my legs.

By this time, I had become medicinally fatigued. Perhaps I did not allow enough time for the medications to work. I simply didn't want anymore.

This ordeal caused a tremendous loss for me as my independence has waned. This gradual decline occurred while I was on the medication. By all accounts, the medication did what it was supposed to do—slow the MS progression. At that point, I realized it was up to me. I decided to let go and let God lead, guide, and direct my path.

***Symptoms of MS depend on the person, the location of damage in the nervous system, and how bad the damage is to the nerve fibers. Some people lose the ability to walk on their own or move at all. Others may have long periods between attacks (remission) without any new symptoms. The course of the disease varies depending on the type of MS. The illness manifests itself differently in each individual.*** —National Institute of Neurological Disorders and Stroke

Multiple sclerosis is a complicated, often misunderstood neurological disease. Its debilitating aspects can leave a person feeling like they've been deprived of their lifestyle, as its onset usually occurs during the prime of their life.

Early symptoms are often ignored or overlooked as normal occurrences. A positive diagnosis can also be complicated and often mistaken for other neurological disorders. In my case, its revelation has led to a whirlwind of decisions and adaptions, all to maintain a good quality of life.

My team of doctors are still my primary line of defense even though I am not on any DMTs. However, I have taken an expanded approach to dealing with my MS. I have involved homeopathic methods as well as consciously altering my eating habits, while listening, reading, and keeping an open mind to all that is available to me.

Fortunately, I never had to give up my job, although I had fallen in the office several times. While it may have been a challenge getting to work, and concern grew for my safety, for me, the effort it took to get there was an accomplishment, a form of exercise.

When COVID-19 hit, things changed, and my progress was hindered even more. Restrictions from COVID-19 were a double-edged sword. I was relegated to a sedentary lifestyle, limiting my physical therapy options. Working from home reduced my risk of falling at the job.

I asked myself earnestly, *Should I give up and give in to what is occurring?*

But I have a zest for life, and I loved mine. I was too young and too strong to be defeated. I made up my mind to make the necessary adjustments as they came. If I truly believed in a higher being, then I would remain hopeful and allow God to help me!

## HOPE: A Personal Triumph

*Healing is the feeling I will get when the Lord is set*
*to move as He proves that with*
*Optimism and faith, I will have the victory.*
*Just wait while I*
*Persevere through this test, only proving my*
*best until I become*
*Eminent, living as an example for others challenged by*
*any personal hindrance. —TPG*

Even with a malady, God has shown me that He continues to bless and heal me. I am blessed with a wonderful husband who supports and believes in me. My mom, brother, and extended family are my support system. My mom in particular gives me strength. We help each other by providing mental and emotional support. At eighty-eight, she continues to exhibit an unselfish spirit toward me and my brother. I am personally better for it. My friends, many of whom date back to grammar school, are beyond compare. My sorority sisters, particularly those who joined with me during this process, are supportive and loving.

There are many who hide behind the veil of a chronic disease, often suffering in silence. The symptoms can be debilitating and embarrassing, leaving a person feeling lonely and isolated. Finding a suitable support group and a caring medical team helps. I have grown closer to the Lord through this experience, often sitting quietly, listening, and finding comfort in knowing that He hears my plea.

I am determined to stay focused and to remain positive. While I did not ask to be a role model and I really don't want to be a poster child for MS, I have accepted my responsibility to be the best I can be. I tell people I don't have to look how I feel as I adorn myself with what makes me happy, just as I did when I was able to walk. Pain has not been an issue for me, but the associated discomfort, spasticity, and numbness can be beastly.

I was previously very physical with a love for dancing. My favorite pastime was actively participating in African dance. Until I can move my feet and legs again to the majestic sounds of the Djembe Orchestra, I depend on a trainer and chair yoga for strength and endurance.

Remaining active and consistently exercising and moving are a MUST with MS. What keeps me happy matters most. Movement is one thing that does it for me.

***Philippians 4:13: I can do all things through Christ who strengthens me.***

The life I had and loved is no longer the same. But I begin every day with a smile, a positive attitude, and the thought that I am a day closer to my goal of standing again, regardless of what the medical establishment states.

It is the God in me that keeps me strong, focused, and determined. I would not have it any other way.

The inability to walk or stand is more of an impediment than anyone can understand unless they are unable to perform those tasks. They are skills that we unknowingly take for granted; the use of our legs is greatly underappreciated. Even menial activities are now unattainable for me. While I've never been ungrateful for the use of my limbs, I unequivocally understand the need to thank God for them now.

I don't view my illness as a punishment for my naïveté but more as a lesson in God's sovereignty. It continues to be a humbling experience. I am amazed at my resilience and how I continue to handle my issues with a kind heart and a giving spirit. Perhaps God is using me as an example for others, showing that He truly lives through me and that through faith, hope, and love all things are possible.

# Finding Love in Unexpected Circumstances

*Porsha S. Harrell*

*"Though He slay me, yet will I trust in Him: but I will maintain mine own ways before Him."*—Job 13:15

As a young girl, you grow up with plans and expectations—thoughts of marriage, children, and what type of career you'll have. While dreaming of what the future holds, you remain in your present reality, trying to navigate through insecurities and uncertainties. This is where I found myself. Although I had certain dreams and expectations growing up, I based my decisions on my current circumstances rather than on future possibilities that might or might not happen.

I never took the time to really think about how my decisions would alter the course of my life because I was so focused on what made me feel good in the moment. Hey, just shoot me. I was a child, thinking like a child, and I wanted what felt good to me. When I accepted Jesus Christ as my Savior, I didn't understand the magnitude of the decision and the way it would shape the course of my life.

In the framed picture in my house, a girl with water-dampened curls clutches a Bible after her baptism. That girl made a decision based on what felt good. I knew that I liked going to church with the other youth and I believed in what I was learning about God. So, I said "yes" to following Him. Little did I know that my yes to Him would be a yes to many unexpected circumstances that would turn out to be challenging. But as I look back, as crazy as it may sound to you, I wouldn't change a thing. So, journey with me as I share how my intentional yes at a young age would help me through an unexpected challenge I never imagined saying yes to.

## AN UNEXPECTED, BEAUTIFUL GIFT

At the age of twenty-five, I had the absolute pleasure of giving birth to a beautiful, unexpected gift in the form of my son. However, I would be lying if I wrote that I had a picture-perfect story leading up to his birth. The truth is I was absolutely miserable. I was making all the decisions that would lead to a baby, yet I was shocked when I actually got pregnant. Without a doubt, I couldn't imagine ending the pregnancy, yet I didn't want a child at this time or in this way.

Even saying this makes me feel terrible because although I love my son deeply, I had always expected to have children within marriage. Not only was I not married, but there were so many other complicated factors surrounding this birth. I carried so much shame and anger for finding myself in this situation. Yet here I was, accepting the consequences of my choices.

There was no reading of birthing books. I wasn't purchasing little things or thinking about a baby shower. I wasn't looking at cribs and dreaming of who my child would become or what he or she would look like. Instead, I walked through this journey just doing what was expected of me in this unexpected circumstance. No matter what I felt about this birth, the mountain I hit next was not one I was prepared for or even wanted.

The day came for a doctor's appointment, and I expected it to be like any other. I was considered a high-risk pregnancy and had different complications, so I was used to more frequent doctor's visits. But this day was different. I found out that my baby had little to no fluid around it. What should have been a regular doctor's visit turned into a hospital stay, in hopes of helping me carry my baby to term. I wish I could say I remembered how many weeks and months I was, but I don't. All I know is, at that moment, it wasn't time. I don't believe it had truly hit me yet, so I lay there with the mentality that this was one more unexpected circumstance. There was nothing to do but roll with it. It was just another burden to carry.

How could I have been so careless and not taken care of the things that could have prevented this situation?

So, I rolled with the punches. I rolled with the punch of being stuck in a hospital bed. I rolled with the punch of eventually having to have an emergency C-section. But then I hit a turn that I just couldn't roll with. I gave birth to a beautiful baby boy who would be mine for only a few short hours. This beautiful baby boy entered this world and left it shortly thereafter.

Gathered in a room with many supportive loved ones, I held my lifeless child in my arms. When they rolled me to my hospital room, there was no baby to take care of. Instead, on my door was a leaf with a raindrop falling from it. Things had gone so fast that once I got to the room, I wanted them to let me hold my baby just one more time. The regret of deciding to let the hospital handle my child's remains washed over me. I didn't see it at the time, but this would be one of God's kisses of love toward me as I would soon realize that there was a mix-up. I would actually be able to have my child's remains rest in a gifted urn baby block in my home. However, that's another story for another time.

After giving birth, I left the hospital with a cesarean scar instead of my arms filled with a little boy. I also left the hospital with my hands holding a grief packet. And just like with other unexpected turns, I rolled with it. I rolled through the memorial service. I rolled through healing from the cesarean section. I eventually tried to manage through life as usual.

Life had changed whether I had realized it or not. I was not the same. I was hurt, I was angry, and I was ashamed. And I carried all of it because I felt it was mine to carry. I spit my anger out on the one who didn't deserve it. Most of all, I pretended I was fine when I wasn't. I pretended through Mother's Day, my son's birthday, and any other life events that reminded me of him. I carried on this way for seven years.

I felt the decision I made got me here. I knew God's Word and I knew in His Word that the circumstances surrounding my innocent, beautiful baby boy resulted from a decision I shouldn't have made. This pain differed from when my father passed away in the eighth year after my son's passing. With my father, I blamed God (I'll share more about this experience later in this chapter). With my son, I blamed myself. I felt this pain was my fault and mine to bear alone. Throughout this journey with my son, I carried shame that was never God's intention. And if I had stayed in that place, I would never have made it to the other side of healing, where God's love resides.

If you find yourself stuck in the same place I lay in for seven years, journey with me as I share three key insights I learned.

## THE POWER OF TRANSPARENCY

Vulnerability has never been my strong suit. I had the mentality that your business is your business. When it comes to life's problems, you let people see what you want them to see, and you carry the real you behind a mask.

However, the truth is: anything that is covered up can't be healed. On the flip side of that coin, not every person or place provides a safe environment for vulnerability. I also learned that not only is it important where you're transparent, but it has to be the right timing as well.

Vulnerability leaves you open. It leaves room for your mind to have you falsely believe that you are now prey to the opinions, shame, and judgment of others. It can make you feel weak and under the control of the person you were transparent with.

I'm not sure about you, but I'm a woman who just recently found out that she is a bit of a control freak and flares up when in protection mode. This means timing is everything. The timing didn't align for me until the seventh year of losing my son.

I am very grateful that I have been blessed with supportive family and friends. Every year for my son's birthday, we got together and did something. However, in the seventh year, something was different. After dinner at Texas Roadhouse, my family and a couple of friends gathered outside. I wish I could tell you I remember the conversation. I wish I could tell you someone said some profound words that led me to open up. But I don't remember one word. I just remember crying in my brother's arms while surrounded by people I love, letting them see my true pain. Not the masked pain I had shown before, but my raw hurt. In that space where they already knew the backstory, I laid a weight down, although I didn't know it then. I wouldn't even recognize it until my son's eighth birthday, but I had laid down shame and anger and picked up peace.

Isn't that just like God? His Word says in John 10:10-11, "The thief cometh not, but for to steal, and to kill, and to destroy: I am come that they may have life, and that they may have it more abundantly. I am the good shepherd. The good shepherd gives his life for his sheep." And Romans 8:1 says, "Therefore, there is now no condemnation for those who are in Christ Jesus." Yes, my decisions led to unexpected circumstances, and I was wrong. But regardless of what brought me there, God's love never meant for me to wallow in that place.

Vulnerability allowed me to replace the feelings that had kept me bound with the liberating power of love. God allowed me to be in the right place, at the right time, with the right people so that I could be the recipient of what it feels like to be vulnerable under His care. Vulnerability under His care breeds forgiveness. Vulnerability under His care brings peace. Vulnerability under His care reveals an indescribable amount of love. I imagine this is what the woman from the Bible, caught in adultery, felt like when she was only left surrounded by the ones who refused to cast a stone. Like her, I was surrounded by people who wouldn't cast stones but simply remained present, allowing me to be vulnerable. This experience led me to discover the power of relationships.

## THE POWER OF BUILDING RELATIONSHIPS, NOT RELIGION

I never placed much importance on intentionally cultivating relationships. While family relationships mattered deeply, they felt natural and effortless—just part of who I was called to be. I wasn't intentional with friendships, though my current friendships inspire me to be more deliberate. The same was true of my relationship with God. Despite my active church involvement—ushering, singing in the choir, praise dancing, and eventually preaching—I wasn't truly intentional in pursuing that relationship.

Through losing my son, I learned that I was practicing religion while just letting relationship tag along. Just like in my friendships, I wasn't being intentional—God was. When I finally did get intentional, you would think that it would look like me telling God just how sweet He is and us walking together hand in hand. But it was nothing like that. After becoming vulnerable with God and feeling so much peace on what would have been my son's eighth birthday, I would be hit with another unexpected circumstance. God would make the decision to take my father. Going through this process, although still a death, looked nothing like it did when it came to my son. I knew I had done nothing wrong, so there was no shame. I knew that this was a decision God had made all on His own and I was angry.

I remember someone asking me to pray and when I did, I couldn't fake it. I told God that me and Him were not on the best of terms, but to please still cover the ones I was praying for and do whatever He sees fit. I know it's foolish, but I felt tricked. God had watched me go through seven years of pain with my son. And just when I had finally found peace, I got robbed of it. Now I had to deal with the loss of my dad. However, I would later see that God loved me enough to not let me carry two heavy weights at the same time.

In that season of being angry with God but being real and vulnerable with Him about how I felt, I learned to love and trust Him. I learned, as Matthew 5:45 says, "He causes his sun to rise on the evil and the good, and sends rain on the righteous and the unrighteous." Through these tragedies, I've learned to share my raw feelings with God, even the ugly truth. Despite everything, I can say to God, "I still don't want to live without You." This honest exchange birthed a real, loving relationship with Him.

## TRAGEDIES BIRTH TRANSFORMATIONS AND TRANSITIONS

I've never been a fan of pain. Who has? As a child, I tried not to do too much that would get me in trouble because I didn't want to experience the consequences of what came with it. I often steered away from taking risks. I found it hard to make decisions because I was so afraid of making the wrong one and having to deal with tragedy because of it. Pain just doesn't feel good. However, through this journey of life, I've gained a different perspective on the significance of tragedies. It reminds me of Paul's story in Acts 27 when he and other crew members ended up on the island of Malta.

Paul had warned them not to sail, but they refused to listen. As expected, the ship hit a major storm. Those on the ship wanted to do what we all try to do when we hit a tragedy—abort the mission. Paul shared that anybody who jumped ship would lose their life, but all who went down with the ship would make it out alright. We later see in the story how the ship breaks into pieces, and those who were saved floated to safety on its fragments.

That's just like life's tragedies. The loss, no matter what it is, has a way of entering our lives and ripping them into pieces. But I encourage you, don't abandon ship. The fragments that are left will transport us to a part of our lives we never expected.

Where Paul and his crew landed wasn't their original destination. They were headed for Rome but ended up in Malta. During this detour, Paul healed the sick, and the island's chief honored them. While their losses couldn't be replaced, they were replenished. They received what they needed from an unexpected place to reach where they needed to be. Our tragedies are transportation to our destined places, transforming us to be ready when we arrive.

I'm not sure who my story may help, but I pray it reaches someone who sees no hope because of their decisions or losses. Through God, there is hope. In unexpected circumstances, you can discover His love, even when it feels absent. I won't pretend it's pretty or feels nice—it doesn't. I'm not always happy with God, and I'm still healing. This journey of healing is lifelong.

I remember a woman said to me that the pain of loss never goes away but over time you learn to handle it better. The loss of my son and father will forever be defining moments in my life. However, through these defining moments, I am constantly reminded of how these life-shaping tragedies have strengthened me and continue to strengthen my ability to be vulnerable.

Those losses have taught me: that walking this journey can't be done without a relationship with God; that having a true relationship with God doesn't look pretty—it can be scary but it's worth it; that tragedies are inevitable whether you believe in God or not; and that my expectation of growth and love under God's care won't and can't be defined by what I read in fairy tales. Transformations can be beautiful shipwrecks when you decide to stay with the Master of the ship rather than venturing off on your own.

So, yes, that little girl who accepted Jesus Christ as her Savior had no idea what life had in store. That little girl has grown into a woman who still doesn't know what tragedies lie ahead, and to say I'm not nervous or afraid would be a lie. However, I will say that the "yes" I gave to God so long ago still stands today. It is because of that commitment that I have the absolute pleasure of experiencing God's love for me in unexpected circumstances.

*Dear God,*

*I come here praying for the person reading this book. I am not sure of the reason why You led them to this chapter or any other chapter of this book. However, I know that nothing happens without Your allowance or orchestration. I am well aware that although we make plans, Your Word serves as a reminder that at the end, it's Your plan that is manifested. If the reader finds themselves in a state of hopelessness, may they be reminded that You are near to those who are brokenhearted. If they find themselves stuck in a place of shame, may they be reminded that there is no shame for those who believe in You. If they find themselves trying to manage the regrets of their decisions and find it hard to accept Your gift of forgiveness and love, remind them that repentance lays aside regrets.*

*I pray that whatever they stand in need of that You fulfill it according to Your will and purpose. May they lay aside what they expected and be open to Your ideas because Your ways are far greater than ours and have the ability to exceed anything we have ever imagined. Allow them to know that even in the midst of what they see as a tragedy, You see an opportunity to show Your power, glory, and unrelenting love. Show them that this part of their story is not the end, but just an unexpected turn toward a life that will still carry out Your will. Allow them to know that Your love for them is great and You have not left them and never will.*

*I love You, I thank You, and I honor You. It's in Your precious name, I pray. Amen.*

# When the Sun Goes Down

*Imogene Van Buren Burke*

*"The Lord gave, and the Lord has taken away; blessed be the name of the Lord"*—Job 1:21

To begin with, I learned early that life was filled with everything from bumps and bruises to death and other incidents that bring tears and sorrow. I'm sure almost everyone has asked God the "Why me?" question. Generally, there is no preparation for it when it comes. When this day came for me, the sun appeared to go down so completely and stayed away so long that it seemed it would never rise again. Despite its seemingly prolonged descent, somehow, I found myself in the pitch blackness of midnight, trying to navigate how I got there. Yet, there I was. *"Weeping may endure for a night, but joy comes in the morning" (Psalm 30:5).*

In 1992, my life was full, beautiful, colorful, and as jam-packed and complete as a brand-new puzzle board. Although my home life seemed to have as many mismatched pieces as a fifty-piece jigsaw puzzle, it fit together as a harmonious unit. I loved life. I loved being a wife. I loved being a mother of three wonderful children. I loved God and the man God gave me. I basked in their love, and all was right in my world. My husband and I ran neck and neck in the race of life, working and attending college.

My life hummed and flourished. It held few surprises. If I could sum it up in just one word, life was good. However, good has a way of going bad fast, and even faster sometimes when death knocks and forces its way in. It seemed to me at times that good was up to no good. What I witnessed when my good had gone bad was that it left deaths, brokenness, illness, inconveniences, and questions in its wake. *"Yet man is born to trouble, as the sparks fly upward" (Job 5:7).*

The bright, windy evening of March 30, 1992, was the first of many experiences of good going bad. That evening, I was told that my only son had suffered irreversible brain damage. He was brain dead. I had sat by his bedside the day before physically numb and white-knuckled, waiting, hoping, and praying for him to open his eyes, to smile, for any sign of life. Yet, that evening, despite all the bitter tears, the prayers, and hope, he remained lifeless.

I sat listening to the faint puff and wheeze of the ventilator manipulating his breathing. The device forced an artificial movement in his chest. At first, I was happy to see any movement at all until the truth of it gradually crept in and spread into the deep recesses of my brain—it was the machine, not him. This knowledge required me to acknowledge and release something I wasn't able to comprehend at that moment.

First, have you ever been so sad, so desolate, and so befuddled that your hold on reality seemed tethered to a frayed thread? At the moment of realizing my son was dead that evening in the hospital, my chest physically ached. I felt as broken and irreparable as the nursery rhyme character Humpty Dumpty after his great fall. It was hard to draw breath, as if I had been pierced by a million arrows and shattered into as many pieces. I was left with a hollow and painful feeling.

While I remember that the day was warm and bright, with a crisp wind blowing outside, I felt a bone-chilling coldness deep inside. The sun of that bright and beautiful day was the only thing that spared me any warmth. So, I soaked it in hoping it would melt that icy feeling as I stared at the still figure in the hospital bed under the oxygen tent. I think it would have been less hurtful if my chest had been ripped open and my heart snatched out whole. Then I would not have experienced this slow-motion breaking of my heart, this incessant pain. Here is where my hope turned to despair. *"But by sorrow of the heart the spirit is broken" (Proverbs 15:13)*.

Later that night, I told my two daughters. To help stop my discomfort and internal hemorrhaging, I enfolded them tightly against me until I felt their protest to be released. I loosened my grip to spare them additional pain. Still, desperate for warmth of any kind, as well as a crutch, I pressed them as gently as I could against that spot in my chest that needed a balm. Only the warmth of their bodies and the steady beat of their hearts helped to stem and cauterize my inner bleeding. Yet, it did nothing to restrict or close the gaping hole in my heart and soul. *"Then Job stood up, tore his robe, and shaved his head; and he fell to the ground and worshiped" (Job 1:20).*

At midnight, I found myself in a deep, dark, and dreary place mourning my loss and wondering, *Why me?*

In the Bible, despite his great losses, Job decided to worship God. In contrast, I couldn't worship God. In those moments, I couldn't even feel God's presence in any meaningful way. Worse yet, I felt angry with God for allowing this to happen.

My efforts were spent trying to draw breath and identify our immediate needs. I focused on everyone and everything around me. I knew I needed God, but for the first time in my life, God seemed distant. In other words, the events of that day overshadowed everything, including God.

I used all of my energy to sustain and nurture the lives of those around me. When I did remember God, I couldn't dwell on Him. In those instances, I believed hearing from God did not matter because I did not matter. I felt like only the lives around me mattered.

Second, following the funeral, I learned what truly mattered. My life's puzzle was forever broken and irreparable. I became acutely aware of the other major symptoms of demise and loss within our family nucleus. After our son's death, I noticed my husband's aloofness and shift away from me. Away from us. Upon closer observation, I started to see subtle, albeit secret, controls designed against me and our girls. His detached behavior presented overwhelming evidence of his physical and emotional withdrawal. He was shutting down and quietly quitting the family unit.

The first great hit to the gut was when he removed all the money from our joint bank accounts. I noticed when I went to the bank the payday after the funeral. I just happened to find out by accident that my automobile and life insurance policies had been canceled. I was also informed several months later that I needed to get health insurance. The health insurance for our daughters and myself had been canceled. Those circumstances caused me to become more focused. I was quite unprepared for the havoc I found myself in. What was worse, our oldest daughter's health was in jeopardy. My grief took a backseat to all the other life events.

Similarly, other breakdowns and issues emerged, particularly in our personal relationships. It appeared my husband had pulled the full mantle of mourning our son's passing over his head like a blanket, completely enveloping himself in grief. Perhaps this was his way to shield himself from reality or avoid confronting our loss. I sensed that he allowed his grief to sever all emotional attachment with me.

To initiate further control, he withheld spousal support, devotion, and intimacy. He similarly minimized support for our daughters.

The widening chasm manifested itself in increased absences. He became an absentee husband and father. A month or so after the funeral, he cut all our joint ties and plans with our families. Everything we once did together—vacations, school, church outings, and functions—were gone. He and I had little to no face-to-face interaction and rarely spoke on the phone.

It became apparent that he only spoke to the girls when absolutely necessary, and when he did communicate, it was abrupt, sharp, and snappy. The blessing was that the girls, so distracted and filled with grief over losing their brother, hardly noticed what was happening around them, and I thanked God for that.

Third, our oldest daughter took our son's death extremely hard. She suffered deep bouts of anxiety. It not only caused her emotional pain, but physical pain as well. I saw how it affected her health and her studies. It was hard for her to function at school. I sent her to school anyway because I did not want her to become aware of what was going on at home. She was very sensitive and intuitive. I needed the girls to have a sense of normalcy. I could see that my youngest daughter handled her brother's death much better. Her grief was apparent, but she was stronger and able to help me deal with her sister's increasing decline. I was eternally grateful that she did not question me, her sister, or her situation.

The girls willingly took all their edicts from me. I was always the overseer, the mommy bear, the constant, the more present figure in their lives. They naturally looked to me for guidance and management. As a matter of fact, prior to this episode, when their father was home from work and college, he was a lighthearted, anti-disciplinarian source of fun. I was the manager, disciplinarian, and provider of normalcy. I recognized our daughters needed routine and was committed to maintaining it.

As our oldest daughter's condition worsened and her sickness grew more evident, I sought God again. *Where are you, Lord?* I wondered. Admittedly, mine was a broken life, Humpty Dumpty incarnate. Isaiah 26:20 says, "*… enter your rooms and shut your doors behind you. Hide yourselves a little while until the wrath has passed.*" This is what I tried to do. All I felt I could do. All I wanted to do. Conversely, I could not go on living like I didn't know God.

For six months, I floundered, struggling to catch my breath and find God. My mental anguish kept me from Him, creating a hit-and-miss relationship. I felt like a shaken carbonated soda, pressure building until I thought the top of my head might explode. Strangely, I wished it would burst open and fly into pieces, if only to relieve the intense internal pressure.

Although I prayed, I was full of unidentified emotions—grief, anger, and hurt. My prayers would sometimes end nonsensically or in rants. I would try, give up, try again and give up again, feeling increasingly defeated. It became easier each time I tried to pray to give up and not try again. My turbulent emotions kept me walking away from God. I comforted myself by blaming Him: *God doesn't care anyway. If He did, He would have been here when I needed Him.*

I had not been back to church since the funeral. I knew I needed to go, but I couldn't. It was as if me going back to church would be letting God off the hook. I wanted to punish Him as I felt He was punishing me. In this limbo, I felt that God had forgotten me and wanted what I was incapable of giving. *"I will test you with the measuring line of justice and the plumb line of righteousness. Since your refuge is made of lies, a hailstorm will knock it down. Since it is made of deception, a flood will sweep it away" (Isaiah 28:17, NIV).* What I didn't realize was that I was already in the testing phase, and God was about to knock down my refuge of lies with His *"justice"* and *"righteousness,"* where my only sanctuary was Him.

On my birthday, June 5, my testing came. When I arrived home from work, I found my youngest daughter sitting on the stairs holding her unconscious sister. I called 911. With a firehouse a couple of streets away, I thought they would be there immediately. When ten minutes passed and there was still no ambulance, God gave us the strength to put her in my car. We headed to the emergency room. While driving, I cried out in anguish, "God, where are You? I need You. Please don't leave me again."

That night, I recognized one of the many angels God had been sending throughout my journey. I realized God had been with me all along, though I was too blind and brokenhearted to see Him. At the ER, my daughter was taken back immediately. Hospital staff struggled, complaining her veins were too small, rolling and resisting their attempts to draw blood or place an IV.

I watched them frantically work around her still body as she seemed to be vanishing before my eyes. Suddenly, a tall man approached and gently lifted her like a baby while he hummed a sweet lullaby. He patted first one arm and then the other, and in seconds he had placed an IV in her arm and tubes of blood lay on the table beside him. He gently placed her on a bed. As he finished, I became aware again of the noise around me. The hospital workers continued to buzz around, prepping her for the intensive care unit.

Once again, I sat white-knuckled, watching and praying for another child. I held her hand and observed the slight movement of her chest, bolstered by the fact that she was breathing unassisted. Not knowing anything else, I expected her to stop breathing at any moment. But she did not. Like before, panic-stricken, I desperately desired to know something, anything.

News did not come until midday the next day. The doctor with her team came to her bedside. She looked straight at me, was professional, and spoke bluntly. She told me that my daughter's condition was grave. As best as I can recall, she said, "Your daughter, if I'm correct and by all indications, has a severe case of Systemic Lupus Erythematosus (SLE). In her present condition, she has perhaps twenty-four to seventy-two hours to live as her immune system is severely compromised. With your permission, I have an aggressive treatment plan that's designed to give her some relief in about twenty-four hours. If I am wrong, her organs will shut down, which will result in death."

I was asked to leave so they could do their work, but I could not. I was told to reach out to immediate family to inform them of her condition. I called her father, as we no longer lived with him. He simply held the phone in silence as I spoke. Hanging up, I was deeply saddened. To extend him grace, I thought, *Perhaps the pain of hearing of the possible loss of another child was too much to bear.* I was further saddened that I had to bear this alone and that we could be dismissed so easily, simply by hanging up the phone.

That evening, the doctor returned and told me that my daughter was still breathing on her own. She said that if anything happened regarding her, the night duty doctor would call me. In the meantime, I left for home hoping for a little sleep. However, after arriving home, I found myself alone, sorrowful, lamenting, crying, and praying, unable to sleep as I relived what I had already lost. Reading normally worked, so I tried to read. I picked up my Bible, but I couldn't concentrate due to my distress. Still wondering why bad things seemed to be happening to me, I tossed the Bible aside. It fell open to the book of Job. Another throw and it opened to Job. Although my eyes went to Job 1:21, I shut the Bible and flung it aside. It opened again to Job 1:21.

Obediently, I sat down on the side of the bed and began reading. I read Job over and over again and felt God's ministration. Each word was succor and salve, as it revealed a little more of God's truth and my lack of faith. Before I began this journey on March 30, 1992, I had developed an attitude of entitlement and self-righteousness. But God—in His infinite wisdom, grace, and mercy—used the Book of Job to restore me. He reminded me that He alone is sovereign. His will for me, for us, is for our good. He cares for us and loves us while we're going *"through the valley of the shadow of death,"* and we are to *"fear no evil"* as our faith rests in Him.

God held me fixed on Job long enough to pour His Spirit back into my broken heart. He showed me that He was my advocate and not my adversary. It was a balm for my soul. God's indwelling Spirit dwells within my heart. As He whispered in my heart, "Why not you?" He also whispered, "Even alone, you're not alone." I wrapped myself in that truth and fell asleep repeating: "The Lord gave, and the Lord has taken away; Blessed be the name of the Lord" (Job 1:21). I awoke feeling blessed and repeating, "I will bless Your name."

I did not know what I would find at the hospital in the morning, but I had a certainty and faith that I had lost at the setting of the sun on March 30, 1992. I was grateful to God that I found it that night as I drifted off to sleep. I knew that if God chose to take absolutely everything He had blessed me with, including my daughter, I would still bless His name like Job. God showed me that an all-powerful God, though loving and caring, is not beholden to anyone or anything. Therefore, *"We* (have to) *walk by faith and not by sight" (2 Corinthians 5:7).*

The words in the Book of Job revived my soul, which was once tethered to a fragile strand of hope and a mustard seed of faith. Job showed me that God had taken from him his entire family, everything, including his health. Yet, during his time of testing, Job never lost his faith and God never left him. Job's *faith* spoke to my spiritual need to call on Jesus when facing the enemy's temptations and strongholds, showing how to remain victorious. God's Word in Job healed my emotional brokenness in ways I'm unable to fully express.

Morning came and I prayerfully made my way to the hospital. I sat watching the still, softly breathing figure before me, thanking God for the privilege to see her live another day. And for the gift of her. With that in mind and a lightness of heart I cannot explain, I sat holding my daughter's hand, praying that God would restore her health. At the same time, I thanked God for who He is. I thanked Him that He gave me the courage and conviction to pray an unselfish prayer like Jesus had in the Garden of Gethsemane—*"Not My will, but Yours be done."*

While I was still praying, my daughter's hand moved in mine. When I raised my head and opened my eyes, she was staring at me. Joy, sweet precious joy, flooded my soul! I cried out loud, "Weeping may endure for the night, but joy comes in the morning" *(Psalm 30:5)*. It was morning at last!

These words written here are easy to say and see now. Although the process of getting them down on paper was more than a notion. In my grief, I heard the deceiver whisper that God was angry with me or was punishing me for reasons of His own. I let the enemy use my selfish self against me. Notwithstanding, the missing pieces no longer felt like empty spaces. In my humble and repentant state, God showed me His goodness, helping me to get back to good. *"Oh, give thanks to the LORD, for He is good! For His mercy endures forever" (1 Chronicles 16:34)*.

All things considered, I know with every setting of the sun that night is imminent. It will come. Likewise, morning will follow. Consequently, some things are changed forever, since life imitates this shattered world. Life gives way to the eventuality of death. What kept me going after my son died was that mornings still came. It also helped that I remembered how my parents described death: like the sun going down. You cannot stop its going down, but if you believe in Christ, like the sun, you will rise again. Death is not the finality of life, Christ is. He holds the keys to death's experience.

In essence, it seemed like my son took the whole family with him to the grave. His passing seemed to put us there with him. Yet, I had two living witnesses of the grace and mercy of a loving God. As after every setting of the sun, He woke the girls and me up with a little more joy and faith each morning.

Uniquely, I was left with two deaths—albeit one was superficial—as I feel like my first love, their father, was unable or unwilling to be resurrected. We mourned his loss with every sighting until his physical descent was completed a few years later. It seems to me that I learned a truth he could not.

The Bible says, "But I do not want you to be ignorant, brethren, concerning those who have fallen asleep, lest you sorrow as others who have no hope. For if we believe that Jesus died and rose again, even so God will bring with Him those who sleep in Jesus" (1Thessalonians 4:13-14).

With that Scripture in mind, I sorrowed in victory, never losing hope, knowing I will see them both again because He who is faithful promised.

# It's Still "Yes" in the Deep!

*Michele Noel-Peake*

"Mrs. Peake, I'm sorry to tell you that Mr. Peake went into cardiac arrest. His heart stopped. We were able to revive him. I'm so sorry. He's been moved to ICU and is on the ventilator."

That was the phone call I got from the doctor on call at the hospital Rod was admitted to just a few days prior for a mini stroke. The day before, he'd lost his ability to talk clearly and swallow.

My heart started racing when I got off the phone with the doctor. I had gone home the night before and was getting ready to go back to the hospital that morning. It was only about fifteen minutes before the doctor called me that I called Rod on his cell phone to let him know I was on my way and he said, "Let me call you back in fifteen minutes." I said, "Ok." Then within that fifteen-minute span of time, I got that call from the doctor. The phrase "Life can change in an instant" is so true. Little did I know how much mine and our girl's lives were about to change.

I immediately began to pray and sent text messages out to close friends and family to start praying as well. We were familiar with needing prayer for Rod, who was in the hospital for a stroke, as he had experienced major strokes a few months earlier and two years prior to this last one. God healed him each time. But this time was different. A cardiac arrest and ventilator was not something we had previously experienced.

By the time I got to the hospital, he was hooked up to all kinds of wires and tubes, the likes of which I had never seen before. It was very difficult to see the person I loved in that state all of a sudden. He was not awake. They had induced a coma in order to hook him up on the ventilator. The ICU physician told me the first twenty-four hours were the most critical for determining if he would wake up. As soon as he said that, I sent a Facebook post out to get even more people praying for him to wake up! Within twenty minutes of sending that post out, Rod started to respond. His eyes opened, he could follow very small commands, track you in the room, and squeeze your hand.

We felt encouraged and hopeful that he would continue to improve. I barely left his side, if at all. I continued to pray to God to heal him like He had done many times before so Rod and I could continue to run our journey for Him.

## THE QUESTIONS

I came in one day and Rod was not as responsive as he had been. His eyes were not moving back and forth anymore. He was no longer tracking those in the room. He stopped squeezing my hand. What happened? They did another MRI to check his brain, and he had yet ANOTHER stroke! A total of about three by then while in the hospital. After a little more than a month in ICU, getting only small movements or reflexes, he was transferred to another hospital to allow more time for his brain to try to heal from the damage caused by the strokes and the cardiac arrest.

As each week went by, I had to watch the man I have loved since my sophomore year of high school, lay in a hospital bed unable to move, feed himself, or do or say anything. At times, it felt like it was all a dream. A nightmare actually. I often found myself walking through the hospital doors and sitting in his room thinking, *Is this real? Is that Rod? Are we really here?* I would wish I was somewhere else. But the reality was, I was in a hospital room. That was Rod in that bed. He was still hooked up to the ventilator. And when I went home, I was going home without him. His truck was there, but he wasn't.

"Lord, what is happening?" I would often ask. Then I would go on, "I know You can fix this. You always do. You did it before. You fixed us as a couple when it was needed and we're better for it. Do it again, God! Heal him. Fix him. Fix us and let us keep fighting for You. We're Your soldiers, Lord! You put us together! Certainly, if You could cause dry bones to live, Rod's wet bones are easy for you!"

After about another month in the long-term care hospital, he was transferred to rehab where he would again be given additional time to wake up. Needless to say, this meant he was getting more and more physically dependent on the ventilator and his lungs grew weaker. He was also becoming more infection prone, and pneumonia was a consistent problem. Yet, I continued to pray and hold onto the hope of Rod one day getting better. I had dreams of him waking up in the hospital, sitting straight up in the bed when I walked into his room, and hugging me.

After a little over five months on the ventilator and in and out of ICU, I remember saying to God one day, "I'm tired." I think what I was really saying was, "God, if You are going to heal him, I need You to do it soon because I am growing weary and I feel it in my body."

The very next week, I got the call no wife of thirty years wants to get. "We do not think he will recover to be able to breathe on his own," I was told. Around that time, his kidneys were shutting down as well. And just a couple of months prior, palliative care had a conversation with me to discuss his options. At the time, I was still holding on to the hope of walking, talking, and laughing with my love of forty years again. The thought of life without my husband never crossed my mind! Sure, we'd had our ups and downs, but God always brought us through TOGETHER. What was happening? I had just lost my first best friend, my mother, the year prior. *God, You cannot possibly be saying You are taking Rod too!? What are You doing here? Show these doctors who You are! Work Your miracle!* I thought.

The next day, after that call and many tears, I did the only thing I knew to do. Things were getting out of my control and I had to SEEK GOD like never before. That Saturday, I asked God to give me a sign of HIS will, not the doctors. God did just that. While with Rod that Saturday morning, I saw sign after sign that he was ready to go. I even asked myself, *Am I holding on to him out of selfishness because I don't want him to go?*

I didn't want to let him go. I knew he would want me to fight for him on the ventilator because we'd had those types of conversations. But had we reached the limit of that fight? It was becoming crystal clear to me that we had. I could only see that because of God orchestrating it for me and using the Holy Spirit to help me make the mental shift. It may sound simple, but that shifting was not easy at all.

That day, once I got outside the front doors of the hospital, I was unable to walk. I started hyperventilating and found it extremely hard to catch my breath. Once I did, I made it to my car and started hyperventilating again. After about fifteen minutes, I started driving home but could barely see past the tears that kept streaming down my face. *Is Rod giving up?* I thought. *How come I can't encourage him to keep fighting?*

That Sunday, I was determined to hear God clearly and directly. I woke up, if I had even slept, compelled to talk to God and listen for His answer. I was determined not to be afraid of what I would hear. "God, I hear what they are saying, but what are YOU saying? Are You going to heal Rod?" God said, "I am bringing him home with Me." I can't explain what I felt, but instantly my response was, "Ok, so what about me?" As if to say, You must be taking me too then. God said, "I am not finished with you yet." Then I said, "Well, are you going to change my name?" Up to that point, I had always heard my name with Rod's—Michele and Rod. Mick and Rod. Rodney and Michele. From fifteen years old to fifty-five years old is a long time.

My heart started to race again as it did the day before when God had shown me signs that Rod was ready to go. I realized it was true. Rod was NOT coming back home to me (us). He was going home, but it would be home with God!

## THE GREAT LOSS

That Monday, my daughter and I had a meeting with the hospital staff to discuss removing Rod from the ventilator after almost six months. We called my youngest daughter, I talked to my dad and a couple of other close family members, and we made the decision. It had been a long, hard fight and I truly felt Rod would have been pleased. I feel like he would have done the same for me had the shoe been on the other foot.

I remember speaking to my Bishop about the decision and he said something that encouraged me. He said, "If you make the decision to remove him, God can still perform a miracle, AND at least now, it will be ALL God." I was encouraged because it was true. God could still perform a miracle. And, yep, if Rod was taken off the machine that was breathing for him, well, we would see. With everything in me, I wanted God to perform the miracle so that Rod could breathe on his own. Do it, God! But, deep down inside, I remembered the Sunday conversation. I'm sure I wanted God to change His mind. And we were about to find out if He would.

Christmas, my favorite holiday, was fast approaching. We had not too long ago had Thanksgiving, Rod's favorite holiday. The date was December 21. Along with me, our daughters—Zarina and Nia, a close friend, and our Bishop watched the love of my life, my best friend, my lover, high school sweetheart, ministry partner, and father of my children peacefully take his last breath and transition home to be with the Lord.

That day was filled with every kind of emotion possible. Too many to explain and even put into words. It's truly something you would have to experience to understand. But the hand holding God did for me and the girls was nothing short of a miracle.

I won't try to explain the hole in my heart that I felt either. Handling my husband's transition to Heaven was far different than my mom's. I was devastated at my mom's passing. I was not surprised, but I was definitely heartbroken that my mom was no longer on Earth with me. She was my first best friend, the woman who gave birth to me, the woman who loved me unconditionally, and so much more. But what I felt and experienced with Rod was, at first, unexplainably different.

I started talking to God immediately with both of them, but with Rod I had physical effects right away, along with the emotional impact. It was too real and surreal all at the same time. I asked God, "Am I physically feeling manifestations of 'two becoming one' when one is about to leave (pass away)?" My best description of this loss is that I felt like a part of me was slowly then suddenly being ripped away from me.

I still can't explain it outside of the whispers of God letting me know that what I was feeling physically was a part of the process. A husband and wife's separation can bring about a type of physical distress due to the emotional and mental trauma. God let me know that when two become one physically through intimacy, and emotionally and spiritually (as husbands and wives do), consequences will be felt.

I believe those experiences vary from person to person because we are all different, with unique relationship experiences. We handle trauma, loss, disappointments, and even love differently. We all have our own personal relationships with Jesus Christ and that will be a driving force in how we cope with life's storms, especially when dealing with the inevitable for the entire human species—imminent death.

Without a doubt, this has been the greatest loss I have ever experienced and I am certain I could not have survived without God Himself stepping down from Heaven to help me through it. I could not have navigated the five-month long journey of Rod on the ventilator in the hospital and not home with us without Him. I thank God HE knew I would need HIM even more to navigate and survive the tsunami which was Rod's death.

God knew before the foundation of the world, before I or Rod were ever formed in our mother's wombs, that this season would be here. He knew Rod would go before me and that I would need to navigate this space, so HE set everything in motion. He knows me better than I know myself, so I couldn't say, "God, You don't understand." I had so much comfort in knowing that God knew exactly how I felt and what I needed. That one TRUTH, amongst others, is what thrust me into HIS arms rather than out of His arms!

Broken, confused, hurt, disappointed, and everything in between, I knew there was nowhere else for me to go. This was something no man, woman, nor I could fix. In fact, God let me know very early on that this would not be something I would be able to ignore and "keep it moving" as they say. I wouldn't be able to brush my feelings to the side either. He let me know that I would need to go through it, not around it. He let me know that HE would be close to me, and He would hold my hand through it if I would continue to TRUST HIM as I had already been doing.

I had just preached Jesus sorrowful in the Garden where He told God, "…nevertheless, not My will but Your will be done" (Luke 22:42), so I knew I would not ask God to take the cup from me, but that I would certainly contend that I could not drink this cup on my own. I would need Him to hold the cup for me as I took each sip. And that's exactly what God did and continues to do.

## THE GREAT GAIN

I have never felt as close to God as I have through the loss of Rod. It's like God would speak to me unsolicited. The morning following the homegoing celebration, I was lying in bed breathing for what seemed like the first time in a while. I recall silently saying to God, *I invite You in*. Immediately God was like, "Where Rod was, where he was headed, and where he is (with Me in Heaven), is best." It's like God gave me the comfort of answering that huge question that He didn't have to answer, but He did.

Even more amazing to me on this journey is that I have felt the presence of God right next to me at times, turning my head as if He was sitting there with me, feeling everything I was feeling and saying, "It's ok. I understand and I am here with you." I believe God is letting me know that He will use my pain for a greater purpose and platform. It will not be in vain. I can't explain the comfort in that, except to say that the Creator of all of Heaven and Earth is with me, my girls, and my grandson. During this season, I couldn't dream of a better place to be than in the very hands of God.

## THE GRATITUDE

The Lord has helped me to cultivate another level of gratitude in this season. One of the last things I recall saying at Rod's bedside before he drifted peacefully into the arms of the Lord was "God, thank You. Thank You that only YOU are separating us." This was definitely after crying and screaming out to the Lord, "What are You doing?! I can't do this! I can't leave him here in this hospital less than a year after leaving my mom. I can't do this again!" Then, the tubes were removed, and Rod peacefully transitioned into the Lord's arms.

My heart warmed over for a moment at the thought that not everyone gets to faithfully live out the vows: "What God joined together, let no man separate." Rod and I got to live that out and more. Literally, God joined us together and now God, and only God, was the one separating us. I could not have felt more grateful for the life, love, family, and growth God had given us TOGETHER. He used us as instruments in His kingdom to help others. Thank you, Lord.

The fact that I am even writing about this journey is all God. I remember having a moment where I thought to myself, *Do I even want to survive this? Can't I just go be with Rod and God now?!* But God showed me not yet. He still had more work for me.

So, I write this open to the destiny that lies ahead for me. God still has kingdom work for me to do, and I am open to allowing Him to perform "surgery" and heal me physically, spiritually, and emotionally. I'm also trusting Him to bring the right people into my life to help me on this journey. I am focused on God and avoiding anyone or anything not meant to weigh in on or impact this new season of my life.

I have also learned in this new season that when it is cloudy and you can't see clearly where God is taking you or how you will make it through, you must hold on to His hands even tighter! I have been squeezing God's hands so tightly while on this journey that you would think I was a pregnant woman giving birth without medication!

I have gained so much from God. And as I approach the one-year mark of Rod's transition, I know I will gain even more. I am nowhere near where I was a year ago. I went from not sleeping to sleeping, from not being able to think about Rod to thinking about him, and from crying to being able to smile. Most of all, I have reached a point where I can be ok with not being ok sometimes, knowing that the Creator of all of Heaven and Earth is going through this with me. In fact, He is the one carrying me.

I have gained so much from God in this season. His Word has shown up in my life deeply and deliberately. Certain Scriptures and biblical accounts manifested in my life. It's like the Word I used to study, hear about, share, and minister to others actually came alive in the middle of my situation and God proved Himself true through it! Biblical accounts of Jesus in the Garden of Gethsemane struggling with His cup now mirrored how I was struggling with mine.

Text like one of my favorites Philippians 4:8, which lets us know that we are to focus (meditate) on the things that are good, true, pure, and praiseworthy, was critical for me. It was so critical because I had to focus on God and not on what I could see or sometimes what I could not see. That was extremely difficult and such a fight for me. But when I did, it was and still is so powerful. It was like I had a new lens on my eyes and a renewed strength to continue to persevere and press on. Scriptures like Jeremiah 29:11 were a constant source of comfort because I truly believe that God does not mean to harm us, but to prosper us.

The HOPE of His Word being true and the hope in His ability to heal me and my girls has been powerful. Watching to see how God would continue to provide, as He said He would in His Word, was something else that kept me going. But perhaps the biggest gain from God has been the depth of my relationship with HIM! It's gone to a whole new level. I really couldn't imagine this journey of such a deep loss without my relationship with God.

He first loved me, then I fell in love with Jesus and this journey confirmed it—LOVE IS REAL. God's love is real. The love God allows us to experience with one another is such a gift. The love HE has for us can take our breaths away. No other love can come close to the love of God when you taste it. "I will never leave you nor forsake you" (Hebrews 13:5, NKJV).

I miss my friend, confidante, comedian, admirer, cheerleader, lover, and husband so very much that I still can't quite express it. When those unexpected moments come over me, God sends His wave of love to comfort me. Now, I can testify from experience that Psalm 34:18 is completely TRUE. *"The Lord is near to those who have a broken heart..."* I don't have enough room to express how other Scriptures have shown up on the scenes of my life during this season and blown my mind, but there have been many. I am grateful for God's Word and the relationship I have with Him!

## I STILL SAY YES!

Over the last several years, I had been a caregiver for both my mom and Rod. I spent much of myself caring for them, in addition to all of my other responsibilities—my girls, business, and ministries. God showed me that it would be imperative to focus more on my physical health than I had been. I was already working on increasing my spiritual health and He let me know I would have to have a better balance.

He guided me to be not only healthy spiritually, but also physically and in my soul—emotionally and mentally. I got a counselor to talk through this journey. I am now pursuing my own health diligently, aiming to be healthy, healed, and whole in spirit, soul, and body for my remaining years in His service. Because He made humans with three parts, I (we) can't neglect one part for the sake of the others.

It's amazing that I sit here today writing this chapter with tears in my eyes but joy in my heart, and I owe it all to God. I still say yes to Him. I think about Job as I write this—not feeling like I'm even close to his righteousness—but, I do understand his greatest fear to some extent and, more importantly, his determination to still rock with God no matter what! I'm trusting and believing in the One that created me and can heal, restore, and put me back together again! And He can do the same for you! Try Him!

# Conclusion

As a child of God, saying "yes" to Him is never a one-time act. Our biggest one-time act of yes is for our salvation—God's FREE gift given to us through His love and grace through faith. This gift becomes yours when you repent of sins, believe Jesus is the Son of God, believe in His death and resurrection, and make Him your Lord and Savior.

If you are reading this, we pray you are saved. If not, we pray you will give God the biggest yes you possibly could—not just for Him, but for your eternal security. God sent His only begotten Son to Earth to redeem us, save us, and re-establish a relationship with us! And He did all of that because He first loved us.

Whether you have read this volume, volume 1, or volume 2 of the Yes, God series, we pray you have found encouragement, inspiration, hope, and God in ways you hadn't before. We want you to take that same encouragement, hope, and inspiration and share it with others. We are fulfilled when your light shines brighter after reading these powerful testimonies of God's goodness, grace, mercy, and favor!

Remember, saying yes to God is a lifestyle. Live your life in the powerful will of an almighty and powerful God, who is always waiting for you with arms wide open.

# About the Authors

*Catherine Ferrell,* a former career banker from Suffolk, Virginia, served as director, senior vice president, and certified treasury manager. She has a true passion for plant-based nutrition and shares her knowledge through blogging, photography, and experimenting in her kitchen "lab." Cathy enjoys exploring new insights and helping others with their wellness journeys.

A recipient of the Barack Obama Presidential Volunteer Service Award, Cathy is also a volunteer Junior Achievement business instructor and travels internationally on mission trips to Kenya, Uganda, and Guyana.

Cathy lives with her wonderful husband and has two beautiful daughters, all of whom love the Lord. Her favorite Scripture is Romans 8:28: "And we know that all things work together for good to those who love God, to those who are the called according to His purpose . . ."

To connect, email her at CathyFFerrell@gmail.com

***Ronda Jennings Morrow*** is president of Jayde M. Schools Incorporated (JMS), a 501(c)(3) nonprofit assisting Washington, D.C. metropolitan area families experiencing a pediatric cancer diagnosis with incidental expenses. Faith and family mean everything to Ronda. She believes being surrounded by a community of love and support is the key to withstanding whatever storms or trials come her way.

Learn more at https://jmschools.org

About the Authors

***Terri P. Guess*** is a professional writer and communications professional who manages Terri P. Guess LLC. She also manages *The Spirit of Essex*, a quarterly magazine for Essex County, New Jersey, that promotes the vibrant arts and history community and seeks to expand opportunities for artists, arts, and historical organizations while increasing public accessibility to their programs.

A graduate of Morgan State University, where she earned a bachelor of arts in communications, Terri also holds a certificate in technical communications from New Jersey Institute of Technology and a mini-MBA certificate in digital marketing from the Rutgers Center for Management Development.

Terri fulfilled a lifelong dream when she became a journalist for *The Star-Ledger*, New Jersey's largest newspaper. Her writing has been featured in *The Amsterdam News*, *Black Enterprise*, and *The Network Journal*. She is a member of Delta Sigma Theta Sorority, Incorporated. Terri lives in New Jersey with her husband, Anthony Smith.

To connect, email her at terripguess@gmail.com

***Porsha S. Harrell*** was born and raised in the D.C. metropolitan area and is the daughter of Angela Harrell and the late Mr. Ricky M. Harrell Sr. She is also the proud mother of her late son and takes pride in being a sister and an auntie.

Porsha graduated from Greensboro College in May 2008 with a bachelor of science degree in mathematics. She currently serves as a teacher, carrying out her passion of working with and encouraging youth and young adults. Porsha is a member of Mt. Calvary Baptist Church of Lanham, Maryland, where she serves, encourages, and uplifts others.

Porsha is also passionate about writing and reciting poetry and fellowshipping with her family and friends. She attributes everything she has to God and takes each tomorrow He grants her as a blessing, allowing her time to be better than she was yesterday!

About the Authors

***Imogene Van Buren Burke*** is a member of Mt. Calvary Baptist Church of Lanham, Maryland. Minister Burke is married to William Burke. They have two married daughters and one granddaughter.

Retired from the federal government as a forensic specialist within the Department of Justice, FBI Laboratory Division, Minister Burke served her entire career in forensics in the discipline of the science of fingerprints.

Minister Burke is a licensed minister who welcomes in-depth conversations about her faith in Jesus Christ, the power and work of the Holy Spirit, the Trinity of the Godhead, and her Christian testimony. She graduated summa cum laude from Lancaster Bible College with a bachelor of arts in biblical studies.

**Michele Noel-Peake** is always humbled when God uses her to impact lives. Whether preaching a message, teaching a class, or coaching a client, she is passionate about using her gifts to help elevate and encourage others.

A five-time Amazon bestselling author, Michele has also won several awards for her public speaking and advocacy work with domestic violence and healthy relationships. She holds a bachelor's degree in business and a certification in lifestyle medicine from Harvard Medical School. She is also a certified life coach and licensed minister. Michele started Michele Renee Consulting to help her clients level up in spirit, soul, and body.

Michele recently lost the love of her life—her co-author, best friend, husband, and high school sweetheart—but not before God blessed them to raise two beautiful daughters and one very handsome grandson, and build a legacy of impactful work and ministry together.

Learn more at www.michelereneeconsulting.com

To book an individual or group coaching session, speaking engagement or FREE consultation, contact Michele at www.michelereneeconsulting.com

Social Media

FB @ Michele Renee Consulting
Instagram @ Coach Michele Renee
TikTok @ Coach Michele Renee
To purchase Yes God apparel,
go to www.yesgodshop.com

## CREATING DISTINCTIVE BOOKS
## FOR LEADERS AT THE TOP OF THEIR FIELD

We're a collaborative group of creative masterminds with a mission to empower leaders to share their unique knowledge, insights, and experiences with the world.

Our expertise bridges the gap between their wisdom and ideal readers—delivering impactful self-help books that inspire lasting growth and change.

**Want to know more?**
Write to us at info@publishyourgift.com
or call (888) 949-6228

Discover great books, authors, and more at
**www.PublishYourGift.com**

Connect with us on social media

@publishyourgift

www.ingramcontent.com/pod-product-compliance
Lightning Source LLC
Chambersburg PA
CBHW072212070526
44585CB00015B/1299